THE

TALK

....

By Dr. Ezekiel Fierce Zeke. Dynamic Public Speaker,
Educator, Motivator, American Activist, Author, and Actor.

Better known as Dr. Zeke, the Educator.
My chief employer is GOD.

PURCHASE BOOK & CONTACT INFO.

Buy this book at amazon.com under "Books," "Kindle Store," or "Audible Books & Originals" for Paperback, eBook, or the Virtual Voice Audiobook. Or, buy the audiobook with narration from the AUTHOR PRIMARILY at BarnesandNoble.com, Nook.com, Audiobooks.com, Audiobooksnow.com, and Kobo.com. And possibly buy the audiobook with narration from the AUTHOR at Hoopla, 3 Leaf Group, Bookmate, My Audiobook Library, Bookbeat, Apple, Radish, audible.com, iTunes, Chirp, and many other online audio book retailers & stores and other places.

If you enjoy this book, please leave a 5-star review and/or a comment.

To book me for speaking engagements, comments, & otherwise contact me or my agent at DRZEKE1@PROTONMAIL.COM AND EZEKIELZEKE@PROTONMAIL.COM, &/OR BY MAILING: 2200 ADEN ROAD SUITE #1004, FORT WORTH, TEXAS 76116.

"I LOVE AMERICA."

My six books titled: 1. *THE TRUTH ABOUT BLACKS AND POLICE BRUTALITY. 2. POLICE BRUTALITY?!? MANY BLACK PEOPLE ARE SO CONFUSED! 3. THE TRUTH ABOUT BLACKS AND POLICE-ENCOUNTERS. 4. POLICE-ENCOUNTERS: WHAT BLACK PEOPLE NEED TO KNOW. 5. POLICE BRUTALITY AGAINST BLACKS?!? THE BIG MYTH AND/OR LIE!* and *6. THE TALK.* All six different books have the same basic exact information and the same exact content. The only differences between these six different books are the book titles and covers. In other words, they are the same exact basic books except for the titles & covers. Also, all chapters and basic information in these six books is also contained in my copyrighted book titled *YES!!! I AM A N.I.G.G.E.R.!!!.* So, if you buy *YES!!! I AM A N.I.G.G.E.R.!!!* once published, you will also have the same basic information that is contained in these six books *as well*, plus the additional information in *YES!!! I AM A N.I.G.G.E.R.!!!.* In other words, basically two books in one.

ACKNOWLEDGMENTS

I just want to thank all of my friends, my family, and supporters who gave their honest feedback on the different drafts of the manuscript, which immensely helped me out to polish all the information. And to also thank all those people who inspired me, contributed to my knowledge, influenced me, and assisted me in the creation of this book – I thank you all from the bottom of my heart!

I thank all of you guys.   Dr. Ezekiel Fierce Zeke

TABLE OF CONTENTS

A QUICK MESSAGE FROM
THE AUTHOR

I am a mature Black-American male. I used scriptures of the Bible, my professional education, science, the law, police policies, public policies, and basic common sense and common knowledge to support all of the serious messages in this book. I have read the Bible's Old Testament in full from beginning to end in sequence on at least four separate occasions. I have read the Bible's New Testament in full from beginning to end in sequence on about seven separate occasions. I have a Bachelor's degree in Political Science. I have my Juris Doctorate Degree in Juris Prudence (the study of law). I researched all the bodies of information and law mentioned above to confirm and to support all of my contentions; and I also applied good basic common sense and common knowledge. I also made every effort to be as accurate as I could within this book. If there are any errors please forgive me in advance.

Some aspects or themes in this book may possibly seem repetitive or redundant. So forgive me for this in advance if that seems to be the case at certain points. However, the repetitive themes were necessary to provide thorough messages. This book has been in the making for approximately one year. This book was written and edited by me, and only me. This book was written from the purity of my heart, and the clear conscientiousness of my mind.

I only mention these things to let the reader know that I have done my due diligence to render the truth and facts within this book; and to also let the reader know that I am not a lazy man. Laziness is considered a sin.

This is a very well-rounded book that can, and will, give you major INSIGHT into all aspects of police-encounters. It will also create major CONFIDENCE to move forward within police-encounter situations.

Thank you for purchasing this book. Purchasing this book is a great spiritual deed, it supports a great spiritual cause, it will save lives, and it will help to bring about more fairness, understanding, and peace and harmony within our great American society. As a great Spiritual People, it is our duty to support all that is GOOD. Purchasing this book is an investment into a better spiritual world, an investment in law-and-order, and an investment into a more prosperous American society. Congratulations!

Now move forward for a Brief Synopsis and for the Gist Of This Book.

By Dr. Ezekiel Fierce Zeke. Dynamic Public Speaker, Educator, Motivator, American Activist, Author, and Actor. Better known as Dr. Zeke, the Educator. My chief employer is GOD. "I Love America."

THE

TALK

....

A CONVERSATION THAT BLACK PARENTS MUST HAVE WITH THEIR OFFSPRING AND YOUNG-ADULTS ABOUT "POLICE-ENCOUNTERS" AND "POLICE BRUTALITY"!!!

A BRIEF SYNOPSIS

MANY BLACK PEOPLE AND OTHERS ARE GETTING THEMSELVES INJURED OR KILLED BY THE POLICE BECAUSE THEY DO NOT UNDERSTAND THE CONCEPT OF WHAT A "POLICE-ENCOUNTER" SHOULD ENTAIL.

THIS BOOK TAKES A PARTICULAR LOOK AT POLICE-ENCOUNTERS BETWEEN POLICE AND BLACK AMERICANS, PARTICULARLY BLACK MEN.

IF YOU WANT TO KNOW WHAT A POLICE-ENCOUNTER IS, PLEASE KEEP READING.

IF YOU WANT TO KNOW WHAT A POLICE-ENCOUNTER SHOULD ENTAIL, PLEASE KEEP READING.

IF YOU WANT TO KNOW WHETHER POLICE ARE WITHIN THEIR AUTHORITY UNDER PARTICULAR POLICE-ENCOUNTERS, PLEASE KEEP READING.

IF YOU WANT TO BE SURE OF WHAT YOUR RESPONSIBILITY IS AND WHAT THE LAW EXPECTS OF YOU DURING A POLICE-ENCOUNTER, PLEASE KEEP READING.

IF YOU WANT TO BE SURE THAT YOU ARE EDUCATING YOUR CHILDREN, YOUR YOUNG ADULTS, AND/OR YOUR LOVED ONES PROPERLY WHEN IT COMES TO POLICE-ENCOUNTERS, PLEASE KEEP READING.

IF YOU THINK BLACKS ARE BEING MISTREATED DURING THE MAJORITY OF POLICE ENCOUNTERS, YOU WILL

PROBABLY BE VERY SURPRISED OF WHAT THIS BOOK ENTAILS, HOWEVER, PLEASE KEEP READING.

AND, IF YOU WANT TO INSURE YOUR SAFETY AND BE IN GOD'S FAVOR DURING A POLICE-ENCOUNTER AND OTHERWISE, PLEASE KEEP READING.

MESSAGE FOR POLICE DEPARTMENTS

SHERIFF DEPARTMENTS, POLICE DEPARTMENTS, DISTRICT ATTORNEY OFFICES, AND OTHER LAW ENFORCEMENT AGENCIES SHOULD FIND A WAY TO DISTRIBUTE THIS BOOK OUT TO THE BLACK LEADERS OF THEIR COMMUNITY, CITY, COUNTY, AND/OR STATE.

ULTIMATELY, THE BLACK COMMUNITY SHOULD BE EXPOSED TO THIS BOOK IF THESE AGENCIES WISH TO HAVE THE BEST RELATIONSHIP POSSIBLE; AND WISH TO HAVE MORE PEACE AND HARMONY BETWEEN THE POLICE AND THE BLACK COMMUNITY IN AMERICA.

IF THIS BOOK IS DISTRIBUTED PROPERLY, THIS BOOK HAS THE CAPACITY TO SAVE DEPARTMENT FUNDS, SAVE MAN-POWER, AND TO ALLEVIATE UNWARRANTED TENSIONS.

THE INFORMATION IN THIS BOOK WILL, AND SHOULD, CERTAINLY CREATE MORE HARMONY BETWEEN BLACKS AND THE POLICE; AND CREATE BETTER UNDERSTANDINGS.

THIS BOOK CAN SURELY SAVE LIVES & DIFFUSE VIOLENCE.

THE GIST OF THIS BOOK

THIS BOOK PRIMARILY DEALS WITH THE POLICE-ENCOUNTER ITSELF, NOT NECESSARILY ANY OF THE AFTERMATHS.

THE SAD NEWS IS THIS; BASICALLY, SATAN IS CONVINCING MANY BLACK PEOPLE TO BELIEVE LIES AND FALSE RHETORIC, WHICH IS CAUSING MANY BLACK PEOPLE TO GET THEMSELVES HARMED OR KILLED WITHIN POLICE ENCOUNTERS.

THIS BOOK AIMS TO DESTROY AN EVIL BLACK PSYCHOLOGICAL PSYCHOSIS ABOUT POLICE-ENCOUNTERS, AND SOME BLACK PEOPLE'S FALSE CLAIMS OF RACISM.

THIS BOOK IS THE CURE!

NOW, ALLOW ME TO GIVE YOU THE BASIC GIST OF THIS BOOK!

IF YOU DO NOT WANT TO BE INJURED NOR KILLED BY POLICE DURING A POLICE-ENCOUNTER, PLEASE REMEMBER THIS, AND HERE THE FOLLOWING CLEARLY:

ONCE A POLICE OFFICER HAS ARRIVED ON A SCENE WITH DUE AUTHORITY, WHICH MEANS HE HAS BEEN CALLED AND/OR HE HAS REASON TO BELIEVE A CRIME OR VIOLATION OF LAW IS BEING COMMITTED, AT THAT POINT, TECHNICALLY YOU ARE NO LONGER FREE TO DO AS YOU PLEASE FOR THAT TIME PERIOD. FROM THAT MOMENT FORWARD, YOU ARE NOT YOUR OWN, YOU ARE NOT FREE TO DO ANYTHING AS YOU PLEASE, YOU BELONG TO, AND ARE A PART OF THE POLICE OFFCIER'S INVESTIGATION. YOU THEREFORE MUST AND SHOULD AT THAT POINT, FOR THE DURATION OF HIS OR HER INVESTIGATION, OBEY ALL THE OFFICERS' REQUESTS AND DEMANDS. KEEP YOUR HANDS WHERE THE OFFICER CAN SEE THEM, PREFERREBLY ON THE STEERING WHEEL, OR WHERE EVER HE TELLS YOU TO PUT THEM. PUT ALL OF YOUR WINDOWS DOWN SO HE CAN CLEARLY SEE INTO YOUR

VEHICLE. DO NOT MAKE ANY SUDDEN MOVES. DO NOT BE UNCOOPERATIVE. TRY TO ANSWER ALL THE OFFICERS' QUESTIONS, IF POSSIBLE. THIS IS OUR DUTY AS A CITIZEN BECAUSE FOR THE DURATION OF YOUR POLICE-ENCOUNTER, BASICALLY, THE OFFICER IS GENERALLY IN CHARGE AND IN CONTROL. THE OFFICER IS TRAINED TO TAKE TOTAL CONTROL OF THE POLICE-ENCOUNTER AND POLICE INVESTIGATION. ALSO, YOU SHOULD NOT BE VIDEO RECORDING THE POLICE-ENCOUNTER, ESPECIALLY IF THE OFFICER TELLS YOU TO PUT YOUR RECORDING DEVICE AWAY. THE OFFICER COULD TELL YOU THIS FOR THE SAFETY OF THE SITUATION, TO EXPEDITE OR NOT TO IMPEDE THE INVESTIGATION, OR FOR ANY OTHER REASON.

AND FOR YOU BYSTANDERS: Just to make it clear, even if you are a general bystander, a husband, a wife, a boyfriend, a girlfriend, a relative or friend, or anybody that is interfering or disrupting the Police Officer's investigation of that person or situation, you can be arrested and charged with "obstruction-of-justice;" as well as possibly becoming a suspect of the potential crime or violation of law.

WE, AS BLACK PEOPLE, CAN NEVER CLAIM "POLICE BRUTALITY" IF WE ARE NOT DOING OUR PART AND COOPERATING AS A CITIZEN SHOULD DO DURING THE POLICE-ENCOUNTER. SO, JUST RELAX AND COOPERATE.

ALSO, JUST FOR THE RECORD: THERE IS "NO" MASS CONSPIRACY (LOCAL, STATE, OR NATIONAL) BY POLICE OFFICERS OR BY POLICE DEPARTMENTS TO INJURE OR KILL BLACK PEOPLE!

POLICE ARE AN ABSOLUTELY ESSENTIAL, INDISPENSABLE, AND NECESSARY COMPONENT OF OUR AMERICAN SOCIETY; AND WE CANNOT THRIVE AND/OR SURVIVE WITHOUT THEM.

SO NOW, LISTEN TO THIS AND HEAR THIS CLEARLY: MANY OF OUR BLACK PEOPLE ARE GETTING THEMSELVES INJURED OR KILLED BECAUSE THEY HAVE BEEN FED LIES AND POISONOUS RHETORIC BY MISLED, CROOKED, DECEITFUL, AND/OR WEAK BLACK POLITICIANS, TREASONIST, RACE-BAITERS, RACE-HUSTLERS, BLACK-OPPORTUNIST, WHITE-OPPORTUNIST, LIARS, BLACK-RACIST, AND/OR OTHER SO-CALLED BLACK LEADERS. THESE BLACK PEOPLE LISTENING TO THESE LIES AND THIS POISONOUS RHETORIC HAVE BEEN MADE TO BELIEVE OR FEEL THAT THE POLICE ARE REALLY TRYING TO INJURE OR KILL THEM, AND THUS, WHEN THEY ARE STOPPED BY POLICE, BECAUSE OF THEIR ACTIONS AND REACTIONS UNDER THIS NEGATIVE PSYCHOLOGICAL STIMULI, IT DOES NOT GO WELL BECAUSE THEY DO NOT FULLY COOPERATE, OR DO THE THINGS MENTIONED ABOVE. AND ON THE REVERSE-SIDE, THIS SAME FOUL RHETORIC CAUSES TENSIONS AND MISTRUST ON BEHALF OF POLICE OFFICERS TOWARDS BLACK PEOPLE, AND IT PUTS POLICE OFFICERS ON HIGH-ALERT WHEN ENCOUNTERING BLACK PEOPLE, WHICH FURTHER INTENSIFIES AND EXACERBATES THE SITUATION CAUSING UNDUE INJURY, UNDUE VIOLENCE, AND/OR UNDUE DEATH ON BOTH SIDES. AND THEREFORE, THE TRUST-FACTOR BETWEEN BLACK PEOPLE AND THE POLICE IS VERY LOW, AND GETTING EVEN LOWER.

AND SADLY, THIS CREATES AN ONGOING AND RECURRING NEGATIVE DEBILITATING CYCLE OF MISTRUST, DISSENSION, AND DISCORD BETWEEN BLACK CITIZENS AND

POLICE OFFICERS IN WHICH BLACK PEOPLE END UP GETTING THEMSELVES INJURED OR KILLED. FURTHERMORE, SOMETIMES POLICE OFFICERS ARE GETTING INJURED OR KILLED IN THESE ENCOUNTERS AS WELL, OR IN OTHER SITUATIONS; AGAIN, BECAUSE OF THESE LIES AND FOUL RHETORIC.

AFTER READING OR BEING EXPOSED TO THIS BOOK, THE BLACK COMMUNITY WILL HAVE NO EXCUSES FOR NOT GIVING POLICE OFFICERS THEIR DUE HONOR AND RESPECT.

NOW, PLEASE MOVE FORWARD, TO THE INTRODUCTION, OVERVIEW, AND WHAT THIS BOOK ENTAILS SECTION, AND THE REMAINDER OF THIS BOOK, SO I CAN EXPLAIN, EXPOUND, CLARIFY, AND PROVE ALL OF THESE CONTENTIONS, MISCONCEPTIONS, AND CONCEPTS THOROUGHLY AND COMPLETELY.

INTRODUCTION, OVERVIEW, AND WHAT THIS BOOK ENTAILS:

WHAT IS A POLICE-ENCOUNTER? BASICALLY, A POLICE-ENCOUNTER IS A SITUATION WHEN YOU HAVE BEEN STOPPED, DETAINED, OR HAVE COME INTO CONTACT OR FACE-TO-FACE WITH THE POLICE THAT IS USUALLY INITIATED BY A POLICE OFFICER.

THIS VERY SHORT STRAIGHT-TO-THE-POINT INFORMATIVE AND EDUCATIONAL BOOK IS A MUST READ IF YOU WANT TO BE IN THE KNOW WHEN IT COMES TO POLICE-ENCOUNTERS IN AMERICA TODAY! THERE ARE TOO MANY PSYCHOLOGICAL POISONS, PSYCHOLOGICAL CANCERS, AND PSYCHOLOGICAL TOXINS WITHIN THE BLACK COMMUNITY IN AMERICA TODAY! BLACK-AMERICANS STOP WRONGFULLY JUDGING OR PASSING JUDGMENT OR CLAIMING RACISM OR PREJUDICE AGAINST POLICE UNTIL YOU HAVE THOROUGHLY READ THIS VERY SHORT STRAIGHT-TO-THE-POINT BOOK. BLACK-AMERICANS STOP CLAIMING "**POLICE BRUTALITY**" UNTIL YOU HAVE READ THIS VERY SHORT STRAIGHT-TO-THE-POINT BOOK! BLACK AMERICANS WE ARE IN DANGER! THIS BOOK CONTAINS SOME VERY STRONG FACTS AND TRUTHS ABOUT POLICE-ENCOUNTERS IN AMERICA THAT YOU DEFINITELY NEED TO KNOW!

BLACK PEOPLE SHOULD ADHERE TO THE INFORMATION AND IDEALS CONTAINED IN THIS BOOK, OR WE AS A BLACK RACE OF PEOPLE WILL CONTINUE TO SEE OURSELVES BEING JUSTIFIABLY DEMISED BY THE POLICE, AND IN OTHER WAYS.

THIS BOOK IS FOR WHITES AND OTHERS AS WELL WHO WANT TO UNDERSTAND WHAT A POLICE-ENCOUNTER SHOULD ENTAIL. HOWEVER, BLACK-AMERICANS PARTICULARLY NEED TO TAKE HEED TO THE INFORMATION IN THIS BOOK! AS BLACK AND WHITE AMERICANS, WE ALL NEED HELP AND MORE INSTRUCTION WHEN IT COMES TO POLICE-ENCOUNTERS! THERE IS VERY GOOD NEWS, INFORMATION, AND EDUCATION IN THIS BOOK! PLEASE READ AND COMPREHEND; IF YOU CAN!

AS YOU READ THIS VERY SHORT STRAIGHT-TO-THE-POINT, YET VERY INFORMATIVE BOOK, REMEMBER THESE THREE THINGS:

1. RULES AND LAWS PROTECT US ALL WHETHER WE ARE BLACK, WHITE, OR ANYONE IN BETWEEN!!! AND AS A RULE-LESS OR LAW-LESS SOCIETY, EVERYBODY WILL LOSE; AND FURTHER, WE ARE ALL DOOMED; AND MOST DRASTICALLY, WE LOSE OUR FAVOR WITH "**GOD**" AND THE "UNIVERSE"!

2. THE UNIVERSAL **GOD** SEES AND KNOWS ABOUT EVERYTHING WE PERSONALLY DO!

3. YOU & I ARE PERSONALLY RESPONSIBLE FOR OUR OWN PERSONAL ACTIONS, BEHAVIORS, SINS &

CRIMES!

AND LASTLY, BEFORE YOU BEGIN TO READ THE CORE MESSAGES IN THIS VERY SHORT INFORMATIVE BOOK, ALLOW ME TO SAY: IF YOU DO NOT LIKE TRUTH AND FACTS, YOU WILL NOT LIKE OR ENJOY THIS BOOK. IF YOU DO NOT WISH TO LIVE LIFE IN HARMONY WITH OTHERS, YOU WILL NOT LIKE OR ENJOY THIS BOOK. IF YOU DO NOT ASPIRE TO BE MORALLY IN-TUNE WITH THE UNIVERSE, YOU WILL NOT LIKE OR ENJOY THIS BOOK. IF YOU DO NOT HAVE OR ARE NOT TRYING TO HAVE A SPIRITUAL CONNECTION WITH A DIVINE-BEING, YOU WILL NOT LIKE OR ENJOY THIS BOOK. IF YOU ARE A PERSON THAT HAS NO MORALS OR PRINCIPLES AND/OR IS NOT TRYING TO GROW AND/OR EVOLVE FOR THE BETTER IN YOUR PERSONAL LIFE, YOU WILL NOT LIKE OR ENJOY THIS BOOK.

NEVERTHELESS, IT IS NOT A MAJOR CONCERN OF MINE FOR YOU TO NECESSARILY ENJOY OR LIKE THIS BOOK. MY MAJOR CONCERN AND AIM IS TO EDUCATE AMERICANS, ESPECIALLY BLACK-AMERICANS IN THIS CASE, TO UNDERSTAND WHAT A POLICE-ENCOUNTER SHOULD ENTAIL SO WE CAN STOP GETTING OURSELVES HARMED OR KILLED.

BY THE WAY, I DO BELIEVE THAT THERE IS A **GOD**. I ALSO BELIEVE THAT THERE IS ONLY ONE **GOD.** THE **GOD** IN WHOM I BELIEVE IS THE ONE WHO I SINCERELY BELIEVE SENT **JESUS CHRIST** TO THE EARTH. THIS IS THE SPIRITUAL THEORY THAT MAKES THE MOST SENSE TO ME.

BECAUSE IF I WERE **GOD**, I TOO WOULD SEND SOMEONE TO TEACH PEOPLE HOW TO LIVE IN ACCORDANCE TO MY WISHES AS WELL; AND TO ALSO MAKE SURE THEY HAD ACCURATE AND AMPLE UNDERSTANDING AND INSTRUCTION.

IF I AM **GOD** AND I HAVE CREATED ALL THINGS, SHOULD I NOT HAVE THE RIGHT TO INFORM CREATURES ON "**MY**" PLANET HOW THINGS SHOULD TRANSPIRE SO EVERYTHING WILL BE PEACEFUL AND THINGS WILL GO AS I HAVE PLANNED THEM? WOULD I NOT KNOW WHAT IS BEST FOR WHAT I HAVE CREATED? THE ANSWERS TO THESE QUESTIONS SHOULD BE A SIMPLE LOUD AND RESOUNDING: YES!!! AND YES!!!

FURTHERMORE, I BELIEVE IN THE SCRIPTURES OF THE BIBLE. I SINCERELY BELIEVE THAT THE BIBLE IS OUR MOST ACCURATE GLIMPSE INTO THE MIND AND WAYS OF **GOD**. BUT MOREOVER, I AM NOT JUDGEMENTAL NOR THE TYPE TO PASS JUDGMENT ON PEOPLE. FURTHERMORE, I AM NOT A RELIGIOUS FANATIC OR ONE WHO IS NECESSARILY CRITICAL OF OTHER PERSON'S RELIGIOUS BELIEFS. ALSO, I AM NOT THE TYPE TO NECESSARILY CLING TO A PARTICULAR RELIGIOUS TITLE SUCH AS CHRISTIAN OR MUSLIM. THESE ARE JUST MY SINCERE CORE BELIEFS.

I LOVE AMERICA. MOREOVER, AMERICA IS THE GREATEST NATION IN THE WORLD TO LIVE IN AND WE ARE FAVORED BY **GOD**.

WHY? BECAUSE AMERICA HAS THE GREATEST EVER-EVOLVING COLLECTION OF WELL THOUGHT OUT FAIR RULES, FAIR LAWS, AND A FAIR CONSTITUTION; WHICH ALL STEM DIRECTLY FROM BIBLICAL PRINCIPLES THAT AIM TO MAKE AMERICA A GREAT ENVIRONMENT AND A GREAT COUNTRY FOR MANKIND TO LIVE WITHIN, IN HARMONY AND IN PEACE. **IT'S SIMPLE, IF THERE ARE NO RULES AND LAWS, THEN THERE CAN BE NO PROSPEROUS AND THRIVING CIVILIZED SOCIETY.** ALSO, I STRONGLY FEEL THAT WHEN THE "BAD" OUT-WEIGHS THE "GOOD" IN AMERICA, THE WORLD WILL BE ON A NEVER-ENDING SWIFT DOWNWARD SPIRAL TOWARDS EVIL, DISSENSION, MAYHEM, DISCORD, AND DESTRUCTION.

NEVERTHELESS, THE INFORMATION IN THIS BOOK IS PREDOMINANTLY ABOUT POLICE-ENCOUNTERS BETWEEN THE POLICE AND BLACKS (AND REALLY ALL OTHERS). SO PLEASE ALLOW ME TO PUT THIS MESSAGE INTO THE ATMOSPHERE TO GIVE THE ETHER A MORE PROPER AND POSITIVE BALANCE.

I AM A MATURE BLACK-AMERICAN MALE. HOWEVER, WITH ME, LIFE IS NOT ABOUT BLACK AND WHITE. BUT RATHER ABOUT RIGHT AND WRONG, GOOD VS. EVIL, JUSTICE VS. INJUSTICE, AND FAIR-PLAY AMONG HUMAN-BEINGS. I AM NOT PRO-BLACK. I AM NOT PRO-WHITE. IF ANYTHING, I WOULD HAVE TO SAY, FIRST I AM PRO-**GOD,** BECAUSE I KNOW **HE** WILL WIN BECAUSE HE IS THE ORCHESTRATOR OF **LIFE.** THEN I WOULD SAY THAT I AM PRO-AMERICAN.

ALSO, WHEN I SPEAK ABOUT BLACK AND WHITE PEOPLE IN A GENERAL SENSE, SOMETIMES I AM INCLUDING ALL AMERICAN CITIZENS IN-BETWEEN AS WELL. THIS BOOK WILL BE VERY EDUCATIONAL AND STIMULATING. PLEASE ALLOW ME TO BEGIN.

POLICE ARE AN ABSOLUTELY ESSENTIAL, INDISPENSABLE, AND NECESSARY COMPONENT OF OUR AMERICAN SOCIETY; AND WE CANNOT THRIVE AND/OR SURVIVE WITHOUT THEM. IN THIS BOOK, FIRST, I WILL START BY ADDRESSING SOME OF THE NEGATIVE LITERATURE THAT IS WRITTEN ABOUT THE POLICE BY BLACKS AND OTHERS THAT I BELIEVE IS UNJUSTIFIED, SO VERY NEGATIVE, AND DOES OUR SOCIETY AND BLACK CULTURE SO MUCH HARM. SECOND, I WILL TALK ABOUT THE ISSUE OF CELEBRITIES TRYING TO GET INVOLVED WITH POLICE-ENCOUNTERS, THE LAW, AND NATIONAL POLITICS. THEN THIRD, I WILL BEGIN TO EXPOUND AND GIVE A THOROUGH EDUCATIONAL AND INFORMATIVE RENDITION ABOUT POLICE-ENCOUNTERS AND WHAT THEY SHOULD ENTAIL. THEN I WILL TEST WHAT YOU HAVE LEARNED WITH THE STORY OF "THE TEN GREEN MEN;" GIVE A BRIEF SYNOPSIS ABOUT A WEALTHY BLACK AMERICAN WOMAN; TALK BRIEFLY ABOUT THE MYTH THAT BLACKS MUST DO A BETTER JOB THAN WHITES; GIVE MY FINAL MESSAGE TO BLACK LEADERS AND BLACK POLITICIANS; GIVE MY FINAL MESSAGE TO BLACK

PEOPLE; AND THEN LASTLY, MY FINAL PERSONAL
THOUGHTS.   THIS   BOOK   WILL   BE   VERY
EDUCATIONAL   AND   VERY   STIMULATING.   I WILL
BEGIN NOW.

CHAPTER 1: NEGATIVE LITERATURE ABOUT POLICE

L iterature should ABSOLUTELY NEVER teach, overdramatize, or imply that Black People should be averse to the Police or towards law-and-order.

Literature should teach that law-and-order is necessary for a civilized society and that the vast majority of Police are not out to physically harm Black people, nor any other people for that matter. If someone is going to create literature about our precious Police, who are a vital part of our civilized society, they should definitely make sure that they understand the law and what a Police Officer's job entails thoroughly.

And moreover, they should be able to empathize and appreciate the serious challenges that Police Officers face just to keep themselves and the public safe. Our Police are precious to us as a civilized society. Our Police are the ones that keep us safe and who protects us while we live our daily lives. Our Police are the ones who protect us while we exercise our daily livelihoods. Our Police are the ones who protect us while we sleep. Our Police are the ones that deal with situations and people that most of us would never want to be near. The Police are the frontlines of our safety as a civilized society. The Police keep us safe from people who do not value life and who would harm society in the most vicious of ways; if the Police were not among us.

People should make sure they know for a fact what they are speaking or writing about before they condemn the Police or our structures for law-and-order in any manner.

To talk or write against the Police without due justification is a VERY DANGEROUS thing to do in a civilized society because precious lives are at stake, and people can and will probably die because of such misguided information. This is certainly not a joke or something to be taken lightly or to be played around with! This is very serious business and a very serious issue!

I WOULD EVEN VENTURE TO SAY THAT IF YOU DO NOT KNOW THE LAW THOROUGHLY; OR YOU DO NOT KNOW THE WHOLE CASE THOROUGHLY; OR YOU ARE NOT ABSOLUTELY SURE YOU ARE GETTING FIRST-HAND KNOWLEDGE AND ACCURATE INFORMATION; OR YOU ARE NOT ABSOLUTELY SURE YOU ARE GETTING THE FULL COMPLETE STORY OR SCENARIO ABOUT A PARTICULAR POLICE-ENCOUNTER OR CASE; AND/OR YOU DO NOT HAVE A THOROUGHLY COMPLETE AND ACCURATE UNDERSTANDING OF THE LAW IN WHICH THE PARTICULAR POLICE-ENCOUNTER, CASE, OR SITUATION ENTAILS; THEN YOU SHOULD NOT PUT ANY REAL CREDENCE TO YOUR PERSONAL JUDGMENT; OR YOU SHOULD NOT PUT FORTH SUCH A STEADFAST OPINION OR JUDGMENT ABOUT WHAT THE LEGAL RESOLVE SHOULD BE IN A PARTICULAR CASE, POLICE-ENCOUNTER, OR LEGAL SITUATION.

But most importantly, and most critically, you should not speak out against the case or police-encounter because your opinion is more-than-likely not predicated on truth and facts. And further, because it does so much more harm to our society, and nothing good comes from it. You should be silent because you are only doing more harm to society by creating more tension.

These uninformed messages and inaccurate steadfast judgment calls create more resentment from the Police, and it further fosters less confidence from the public for the Police. It is simply not helpful. And believe it or not, it costs lives in the short and long term, because when people are misled about the law and the Police; or are suspicious and feel they cannot trust the Police; and/or feel that Police are trying to do them harm, it creates a false hysteria and situation on both sides that can end with deadly or physically harmful consequences. I see this starting to happen more often today. SO PLEASE, if you do not know what you are speaking or writing about thoroughly, keep your opinions to yourself. AGAIN, people's lives are at stake and it does way more harm than good.

Furthermore, literature should not be written to poison the minds of our precious black youth into thinking that the Police are their enemies and that they are out to harm or kill them. This kind of literature or outlandish talk creates a false hysteria and fear in the minds of our precious youth and can ultimately cause them to make a mistake because of nervousness or disillusion when they encounter the Police. So many Black so-called leaders and other Black people do not understand that when they tell the black youth that the Police are out to harm or kill them, it creates a greater potential for harm or death towards the black youth when a police-encounter does occur. Because when people are in fear or in hysteria, they are not able to comprehend as well, and they are more prone to make a mistake during the police-encounter.

Also, some Blacks say that most Blacks fear the Police. I do not agree that most Blacks fear the Police, nor do I think that the Police are out to do Blacks harm. If Blacks do fear the Police, for the most part, it is misguided fear based on false premises.

Any Literature that creates false hysteria between citizens (black or white) and the police should be dismissed and relegated out of mainstream America. What we should be doing is creating an understanding and a rapport between the Police and Black citizens to be able to foster a better relationship between the two; which is my aim here. I certainly do not fear the Police. I know that Police are here to keep law-and-order and to protect the general public, and me, if I am following the law. For anyone to insinuate that Cops are intentionally raining down terror on Black people; and that Cops deliberately shoot Black people for no cause on a regular basis is irresponsible, and it is a falsity that should be immediately challenged, disputed, disrupted, diffused, and dismissed. **THIS TYPE OF RHETORIC ONLY ADDS FUEL TO AN ALREADY DECEITFUL FIRE.**

BOTTOM LINE: MAKING COMMENTS IN GENERAL THAT ARE ADVERSE TO POLICE WITHOUT ANY JUST MERIT IS VERY DAMAGING TO THE FABRIC OF OUR SOCIETY AND MUST BE CONDEMNED SWIFTLY, IN A MAJOR WAY. MAKING BLACK PEOPLE FEEL THAT ALL POLICE OFFICERS ARE OUT TO DO THEM HARM WITHOUT ANY SUBSTANTIAL OR VERY CREDIBLE EVIDENCE IS VERY IRRESPONSIBLE, UNPATRIOTIC, UN-AMERICAN, AND IT CREATES MORE DISCORD AND DISSENSION IN OUR GREAT AMERICAN SOCIETY.

PLEASE SEE THE FULL COMPLETE SECTION DEDICATED TO POLICE-ENCOUNTERS BELOW FOR FURTHER CRITICAL INFORMATION ON THIS ISSUE.

CHAPTER 2

UNINFORMED AND IGNORANT CELEBRITIES

F urthermore, I see some uninformed and ignorant actors, entertainers, rappers, comedians, athletes, and other Black and White celebrities and others who also try to engage in national politics or in cases involving police-encounters and other national issues. When I use the word ignorant, I am not using this word in a derogatory or demeaning sense towards anyone. I am using the word in its rawest sense. To be Ignorant simply means that one does not know, or one is unaware or uninformed. **MOST OF THESE CELEBRITIES DO NOT FULLY UNDERSTAND THE LAW, AND/OR DO NOT FULLY UNDERSTAND WHAT DUE-PROCESS ENTAILS, AND/OR DO NOT FULLY UNDERSTAND CRIMINAL OR CIVIL PROCEDURE, AND/OR DO NOT FULLY UNDERSTAND HOW POLICE-ENCOUNTERS SHOULD WORK. MOST OF THEM HAVE NO BACKGROUND OR EDUCATION IN LAW OR POLITICS.**

I know many of them mean well, or don't mean any harm, and/or really believe what they are saying is right. However, if one does not know what one is talking about thoroughly, one should not voice their opinion, or at the least, not a steadfast opinion; because it does way more harm than good in law and in national politics.

WHEN ONE TALKS ABOUT POLICE-ENCOUNTERS OR NATIONAL POLITICS, ONE IS TALKING ABOUT MATTERS THAT AFFECT MANY LIVES. CELEBRITIES HAVE A GREATER RESPONSIBILITY BECAUSE WHAT THEY SAY AFFECTS MANY LIVES. SO, TO TALK ABOUT SUCH TOPICS SHOULD BE APPROACHED WITH EXTREME CAUTION, ESPECIALLY IF ONE DOES NOT UNDERSTAND THE TOPIC THOROUGHLY. LAW, POLICE-ENCOUNTERS, AND/OR POLITICS ARE NOT EASY SUBJECTS TO UNDERSTAND AND GRASP. CERTAINLY ONE CANNOT GRASP THEM AT A WHIM. FURTHERMORE, MANY CELEBRITIES DO NOT EVEN KNOW OR UNDERSTAND WHAT A SOUNDBITE IS AND/OR HOW SOUNDBITES CAN BE SPUN AND/OR MISREPRESENTED.

For some celebrities to get involved is like someone stepping into someone else's chosen profession or craft that has no clue or experience; however, they are trying to tell you what you should be doing within your own profession or craft. You would not like that. Would you? That would probably make you see them as ignorant and uninformed. You would shun them for sure and would not appreciate their presence and uneducated opinions.

Well, the same thing goes for those celebrities who engage in the law and politics, or cases, or police-encounters that they do not fully understand or do not have experience in. These Celebrities should stick to their professions and/or crafts and keep their mouths closed if they are not totally sure what they are expounding upon. Again, the Celebrity is doing WAY more damage to people than good for the larger society when they act in this manner. They should stay in their lane of life.

Furthermore, Celebrities would save themselves a lot of grief, anxiety, and unnecessary emotional turbulence if they would do so. It is not a celebrity's battle to fight and celebrities are not equipped. They should not stress themselves out over things they do not thoroughly understand. This is why GOD grants other people gifts, talents, and professional skills to deal with things that you might not quite be able to. Some of these celebrities are crying for all the wrong reasons. Some are supporting all the wrong people, the wrong principles, the wrong values, and the wrong causes. This will hurt us all in the long term. However, some of these celebrities may be doing it for monetary gain or personal recognition which is moreso disturbing. It is wrong to be selfish and self-centered.

Celebrities have the power to influence many people in masses to believe that racism is more prevalent than it really is. This hurts us as a people and hurts race-relations in America and in the world. Celebrities' power and influence rubs off on other middle-class and poor Blacks and they feel that racism is very alive and well to a degree that it is not.

Therefore, celebrities have a much greater responsibility for what they say and for the decisions that they make because it influences other people in masses. GOD will hold them/us more responsible. THESE TYPES OF UNWARRANTED STATEMENTS ADD TO SATAN'S REPERTOIRE AND BAG OF TRICKS TO KEEP US DIVIDED AND DISTRUSTFUL OF ONE-ANOTHER, AND TO KEEP THE HORRIBLE LIE OF RACISM AND THE HATE THAT IT BELLOWS ALIVE. PLEASE, LET'S CLEAN IT UP. DO NOT BE SELFISH AND SELF-CENTERED.

THUS, IF A CELEBRITY TRULY CARES ABOUT OUR COUNTRY, THEY WOULD KEEP THEIR MOUTH CLOSED IF THEY ARE NOT ABSOLUTELY SURE ABOUT THE TOTALITY OF WHAT THEY ARE SPEAKING ABOUT BECAUSE THEY ARE CAUSING HARM TO PEOPLE. And really, it shows that most of them do not clearly understand what they are saying, based on current law, police-encounter situations, and politics. This goes for football celebrities, actors, entertainers, rappers, comedians, NBA players, athletes, tennis stars, and/or any other Black or White celebrity that is not fully informed and does not fully understand the particular rules and laws of that particular discipline; or has not had time to get all the facts and evidence of a specific case or police-encounter. If they continue to do this, they certainly do not have the best interest of the nation as their primary concern. So please, do the right thing.

Therefore, people, especially celebrities, since celebrities have a greater effect on people's thinking, should never speak against the Police if they do not fully understand the law and what the rules and law is for police-encounters. A prime example of today is Colin Kaepernick. Colin Kaepernick probably does not fully understand the law nor fully understand police-encounters. I believe Colin means well. I do not think Mr. Kaepernick means to do any harm to our Country.

However, I sincerely believe that he does not fully understand what the basic rules are within police-encounters. He should stick to football because I sincerely believe his judgment is wrong about the law in many of these police-encounter cases. If Kaepernick fully understood what police-encounters should entail, based on the law, he would probably change his view on most of these police-encounters because in many of these cases the citizens have been in the wrong.

I AM FOR JUSTICE. I AM FOR PROSECUTING CROOKED POLICE AND AGAINST POLICE WHO DO NOT FOLLOW OR RESPECT THE LAW OR THEIR DUTIES. HOWEVER, ON THE FLIP-SIDE, I AM EQUALLY AGAINST CRIMINALS AND OTHERS WHO BREAK THE LAW. CRIMINALS SHOULD BE PROSECUTED AS WELL WHEN THEY BREAK THE LAW AND/OR DO NOT ACT APPROPRIATELY DURING POLICE-ENCOUNTERS. I am certainly for people obeying the law within police-encounters.

WHAT I HAVE NOTICED IS THAT MANY PEOPLE DO NOT FULLY UNDERSTAND WHAT A CITIZEN MUST DO DURING POLICE-ENCOUNTERS, AND THAT IS CREATING THE PROBLEMS. Most of, but not all, of the questionable police-encounters that I have seen, the Police have been in the right. In most of these cases, the Police have only been doing their job, and most of the citizens that I have seen in these police-encounters have been in the wrong. People should recognize that we need our police.

IF PEOPLE FULLY UNDERSTOOD THE LAW WHEN IT COMES TO POLICE-ENCOUNTERS THEY WOULD SEE THAT IN MOST OF THESE CASES, BUT MAYBE NOT ALL, THE POLICE ARE WITHIN THEIR LEGAL RIGHTS IN ACCORDANCE WITH THE LAW. **THIS IS EXACTLY WHY I WROTE THIS BOOK ON THIS ISSUE TO GIVE PEOPLE A BETTER UNDERSTANDING ABOUT POLICE-ENCOUNTERS AND THE LAW. SO I SAY, BE CAREFUL WHAT YOU WISH FOR BECAUSE WE CERTAINLY NEED OUR POLICE. IN THIS DAY AND TIME, SOONER OR LATER, YOU WILL PROBABLY NEED THE POLICE YOURSELF.**

Again, it seems that some people would support protecting the criminal before they protect the Police because they do not fully understand the law when it comes to police-encounters. Therefore, they believe that the Police are wrong when actually the Police are right. BUT MOST IMPORTANTLY, I TRULY BELIEVE MOST AMERICANS WANT WHAT IS BEST FOR OUR COUNTRY, BUT SOME OF US ARE JUST MISLED AND MISS-EDUCATED. THIS IS EXACTLY WHY I AM WRITING THIS BOOK. PLEASE CONTINUE.

CHAPTER 3: ALL CITIZENS MUST COOPERATE WITH POLICE OFFICERS "INCLUDING BLACKS"

WHAT IS A POLICE-ENCOUNTER?

BASICALLY AGAIN, A POLICE-ENCOUNTER IS A SITUATION WHEN YOU HAVE BEEN STOPPED, DETAINED, OR HAVE COME INTO CONTACT OR FACE-TO-FACE WITH THE POLICE THAT IS USUALLY INITIATED BY A POLICE OFFICER.

ALL CITIZENS MUST COOPERATE WITH POLICE OFFICERS, INCLUDING BLACKS, BECAUSE THERE MUST BE LAW-AND-ORDER IN A CIVILIZED SOCIETY.

THE KEY TO SOLVING THE SO-CALLED "POLICE BRUTALITY" AND/OR THE SO-CALLED "POLICE MISCONDUCT" PROBLEM WITHIN THE BLACK COMMUNITY IS VERY SIMPLE. EACH PARTY (THE BLACK CITIZEN AND THE POLICE OFFICER) MUST UNDERSTAND WHAT THEIR RESPECTIVE ROLES ARE DURING A POLICE-ENCOUNTER. I USE THE TERM "SO-CALLED" BECAUSE I TRULY BELIEVE IT IS MUCH LESS OF A PROBLEM THAN MANY OF US BLACKS MAY THINK, ONCE WE UNDERSTAND POLICE-ENCOUNTERS. NEVERTHELESS, THE KEY TO SOLVING THE SO-CALLED "POLICE BRUTALITY" AND/OR THE SO-CALLED "POLICE MISCONDUCT" PROBLEM IS AGAIN, THE BLACK CITIZEN MUST UNDERSTAND WHAT HIS ROLE IS, AND THE POLICE OFFICER MUST UNDERSTAND WHAT HIS ROLE IS.

ONCE THESE RESPECTIVE ROLES ARE FULLY UNDERSTOOD, THIS WILL SOLVE MUCH OF THE PROBLEM, OR AT THE LEAST IT WILL STOP MUCH OF THIS UNSUBSTANTIATED FALSE RHETORIC CREATED BY BLACKS, CELEBRITIES, AND SO-CALLED BLACK LEADERS. AND I WILL SAY IT ONCE AGAIN; EVERY CIVILIZED SOCIETY MUST HAVE RULES, LAWS, AND REGULATIONS TO BE AT PEACE AND TO LIVE IN HARMONY TOGETHER. THE GOVERNMENT AND THE POLICE ARE A NECESSARY COMPONENT TO THIS ORDER.

THE POLICE, WHEN ENGAGING CORRECTLY, SERVES AS SORT OF A "REFEREE" OR "UMPIRE" IN THE STREETS AND IN THE PUBLIC WITHIN A CIVILIZED SOCIETY TO ENFORCE THE CURRENT LAW, TO KEEP PEACE, TO PROMOTE FAIRNESS, TO PROTECT THE GENERAL PUBLIC, TO SERVE THE PEOPLE WHO ARE ON THE SIDE OF JUSTICE AND THE LAW, AND IN KEEPING PEOPLE ABLE TO LIVE IN HARMONY WITH ONE-ANOTHER.

ANOTHER WAY TO SAY THIS IS: THE POLICE ARE THE REFEREES OR UMPIRES ON THE STREETS AND IN THE PUBLIC, BUT THE JUDGES ARE THE REFEREES AND THE UMPIRES IN THE COURTS. The Justices and Judges have the final decree in our American system. LAW-AND-ORDER IS AN ABSOLUTE NECESSITY TO ACCOMPLISH A CIVILIZED SOCIETY. NOT HAVING LAW-AND-ORDER LEADS TO ANARCHY, CHAOS, MAYHEM AND TREACHERY. THIS LEADS TO A SOCIETY MORE PRONE TO DO MORE EVIL. LAW-AND-ORDER LEADS A SOCIETY TO BE MORE PRONE TO DO MORE GOOD AND TO EMBRACE GOODWILL.

I DO NOT KNOW ABOUT YOU, BUT I DO NOT WANT TO SEE AMERICA BECOME LIKE MANY OTHER COUNTRIES THAT I HAVE SEEN THAT ARE FULL OF CHAOS, ANARCHY, MAYHEM AND TREACHERY. WE NEED TO CERTAINLY APPRECIATE AND THANK GOD FOR AMERICA.

PHOTOS OF DR. MARTIN LUTHER KING JR. AND HIS WIFE CORETTA SCOTT KING

The late great civil rights leader and minister Dr. Martin Luther King Jr. was a major proponent of obeying the law. Unless of course, he thought it was an unjust, evil, or morally wrong law. Nevertheless, if Dr. King did break a law that he considered unjust, he was always willing to accept whatever punishment the penalty entailed in a peaceful and civilized manner.

In a letter from a Birmingham jail in 1963, Martin Luther King Jr. wrote "One has not only a legal but a moral responsibility to obey just laws. Conversely, one has a moral responsibility to disobey unjust laws." (— Martin Luther King, Jr., Letter from Birmingham Jail).

This was written in 1963 when America did have some laws that were considered unjust by King and some other Blacks. However, today, in 2021, most, if not all of our laws are just, fair, and apply to all the same in most cases. For sure there are no laws that discriminate or that apply to different races differently.

Dr. Martin Luther King Jr. also stated, "Please be peaceful. We believe in law and order. We are not advocating violence, I want you to love your enemies... for what we are doing is right, what we are doing is just -- and God is with us." This further substantiates that Dr. King was a firm believer in law-and-order and in obeying and respecting the law of the land.

PHOTOS OF MALCOLM X

The late great controversial Black leader known as Malcolm X was also a major proponent of obeying the law. Of course Malcolm X also fought against unjust laws and unjust treatments against Blacks. But, he too was always willing to accept the penalty when he would break the law.

Malcolm X once said in part "...Our religion teaches us to be intelligent. Be peaceful, be courteous, obey the law, respect everyone; but if someone puts his hand on you, send him to the cemetery. That's a good religion."

This may seem extreme to us today, but this was at a time when some Blacks were being mistreated, hung, shot, and killed by White extremist. At this particular time, Malcolm X was advocating self-defense to protect himself and his followers. But, the point is, Malcolm X acknowledged that obeying the law was the right thing to do under most circumstances.

Malcolm X would say "Be peaceful, be courteous."

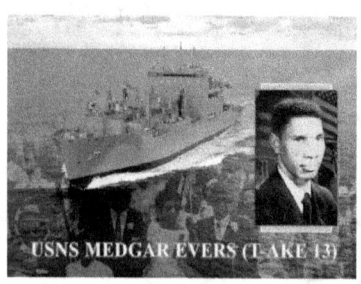

PHOTO OF MEDGAR WILEY EVERS

Furthermore, the late great civil rights activist and NAACP state field secretary and World War II Army veteran, known as Medgar Wiley Evers was a major proponent of obeying the law as well.

PHOTOS OF RONALD WILSON REAGAN AND HIS WIFE NANCY DAVIS REAGAN. MICHAEL JACKSON IN 3RD PHOTO.

Ronald Reagan said "We must reject the idea that every time a law's broken, society is guilty rather than the lawbreaker. It is time to restore the American precept that each individual is accountable for his actions." Reagan Further stated, "Freedom prospers when religion is vibrant and the rule of law under God is acknowledged."

The point I am making here is this: if there are no laws, there is no civilized society, and therefore we all perish. Most great leaders, Black and White, recognize this as a first and foremost component of any civilized society. No rules and laws, no civilized society. Also, the information written here is not to create fear to make sales. This is a sincere rendition and educated proclamation to educate Blacks and others on police-encounters only.

I am a Black Male. So, I certainly understand Black Peoples frustration when it comes to this issue. However, we all must do our part, Black and White, Police and Citizen. The Black-American must do his or her part and the Police Officer must do his or her part. This ultimately starts by people understanding the roles within the police-encounter itself. Once we understand the roles within the police-encounter we can then intelligently look at each police-encounter and determine who is basically following the law or procedures, and who is at fault. It really is just that simple.

AS A BLACK PERSON, IT REALLY SADDENS ME THAT SO MANY BLACK PEOPLE HAVE SUCH A VERY MISLED PERCEPTION AND A VERY MISLED UNDERSTANDING OF THE ROLES OF THE POLICE WITHIN POLICE-ENCOUNTERS. FURTHERMORE, IT SADDENS ME BECAUSE THEY HAVE SUCH A NEGATIVE PERCEPTION OF THE POLICE. It is this lack of understanding, these mislead perceptions, and these misconstrued judgments on behalf of Blacks, which is causing our injuries and/or our demise. This is why this section or chapter of the book is so important to me. My goal in this section is to try to bridge-the-gap, for the better, between us Blacks and the Police, and to create more peaceful police-encounters.

Based on some of these misconceptions, misleading perceptions, and mislead understandings, many Black parents have taught their kids in a misguided manner, simply because they do not fully understand police-encounters. Our children are our most delicate and most precious possessions. Our children are delicate and are very susceptible to trauma. This miss-education about police-encounters is causing our Black children and our Black youth to live in unwarranted fear and unsubstantiated hysteria because they think that the Police and White People hate them. These kinds of teachings usually put the Police Officer in a dark light in the child's mind. It teaches the child that the Police Officer is a bad person and that he is more-likely the enemy to the child or young adult; instead of teaching that the Police Officer is their friend.

This is very bad for our children.

This kind of rhetoric or teachings to our children usually traumatizes them for life; and it creates unnecessary and false paranoia in the mind of the child and young adult. This is horrible for our children and it further creates a false hysteria, a false illusion, a false out-look, and dampened hopes. And thus, our children grow up in unwarranted fear with a false sense of reality about the police and about American life. This seems to be a recurring problem within some of the Black community. If you are teaching your children to fear the Police in this manner, you are certainly doing your child a disservice and limiting their possibilities of living prosperously and having a successful life in America; or at the least disallowing them to know the true reality of law-and-order and what the Police roles are. This certainly sets your child up for failure in society because it creates a warped view of reality in America. The parent that does this should surely be embarrassed. I will prove my point shortly.

I have personally experienced traumas in my youth that still affect me as an adult to this very day. Therefore, I know from experience what I am speaking about. I am sure others reading this material have experienced childhood traumas as well. So, let's start protecting our children by telling them the truth and giving them proper instructions when it comes to police-encounters. In this way, they can grow and evolve in American life and become productive, successful, and happy law-abiding citizens. This is truly what you want to see for your offspring.

BUT AGAIN, THERE IS TOO MUCH UNSUBSTANTIATED HYSTERIA CREATED IN THE BLACK COMMUNITY TO KEEP UNWARRANTED FEAR ALIVE.

> In Matthew chapter 18 verse 5 JESUS says "And any of you who welcomes a little child like this because you are mine, is welcoming me and caring for me. But if any of you causes one of these little ones who trusts in me to lose faith, it would be better for you to have a rock tied to your neck and be thrown into the sea." Luke 17 verses 2 and 3 says "...he would be far better off than facing the punishment in store for those who harm these little children's souls. I am warning you!"

SO, YOU PARENTS, PLEASE PAY CLOSE ATTENTION TO THIS SECTION IN THIS BOOK IF YOU TRULY WANT TO PROPERLY EDUCATE YOUR CHILDREN ABOUT POLICE-ENCOUNTERS. THIS WILL KEEP YOUR CHILD FROM EXPERIENCING UNNECESSARY TRAUMA, UNWARRANTED FEARS, UNWARRANTED ANXIETY, UNNECESSARY PARANOIA, AND TO ULTIMATELY ENSURE THEY AVOID PHYSICAL HARM TO THEMSELVES DURING A POLICE-ENCOUNTER. REMEMBER, JESUS SAID THOSE WHOM HARM OR MISLEADS A CHILD IS HARMING HIM.

ALSO, I HAVE SEEN MANY BLACK PEOPLE, WHITE

PEOPLE, AND OTHERS, ENCOUNTERING THE POLICE BEING COMBATIVE, UNCOOPERATIVE, DISRESPECTFUL, UGLY, NASTY, AND SOMETIMES JUST PLAIN REBELLIOUS FOR NO APPARENT REASON. SUCH UGLINESS IS NEITHER WARRANTED NOR JUSTIFIED. REALLY, IT IS JUST UNNECESSARY. I ALSO SEE THESE SAME TYPES OF PEOPLE ACT AS THOUGH THEY KNOW THE LAW, WHEN APPARENTLY IT IS QUITE CLEAR THAT THEY DO NOT. PLEASE ALLOW ME TO GIVE YOU SOME GOOD ADVICE, AND THAT IS AS FOLLOWS:

IF YOU DO NOT KNOW THE LAW EXACTLY; PLEASE JUST OBEY THE POLICE OFFICER AND SAVE YOUR GRIEVANCES AND COMPLAINTS FOR THE COURT. YOU WILL PROBABLY HAVE MUCH FEWER PROBLEMS WITHIN THE POLICE-ENCOUNTER THIS WAY.

I see some people claim that the Police are harassing them when the Police are only trying to do their sworn duties. Sometimes it is just too ridiculous how some people react to the Police. Sometimes they are very disrespectful for no reasons at all. I have seen too much unnecessary stupidity and disrespect towards police.

IT SEEMS AS THOUGH SOME BLACKS, WHITES, AND OTHERS WOULD CONDONE A LAWLESS SOCIETY; A SOCIETY THAT IS CHAOTIC WITH NO RULES AND NO LAWS. I AM HERE TO TELL YOU, GOD DOES NOT CONDONE NOR SUPPORT THIS PERSPECTIVE OR PHILOSOPHY. GOD, AND HIS SON JESUS THE CHRIST, ARE THE SUPREME AND PERFECT ARCHITECTS AND ENGINEERS OF JUSTICE, FAIRNESS, AND LAW-AND-ORDER. THUS, GOD IS AGAINST THIS FOUL RHETORIC AND SO AM I. I ALWAYS STRIVE TO BE ON THE

WINNING TEAM. I DO NOT FIGHT AGAINST THE GRAIN. GOD'S ORDER IS THE WINNING TEAM AND THE WINNING HAND. FIGHTING AGAINST GOD IS TO FIGHT AGAINST THE GRAIN, YOU ARE GOING TO LOSE.

FURTHERMORE, PEOPLE WHO PROTEST THE POLICE SHOULD BE CAREFUL ABOUT WHAT THEY ARE PROTESTING FOR BECAUSE THEY MAY BE PROTESTING FOR THE WRONG BEHAVIOR. IN OTHER WORDS, WE NEED OUR POLICE. KEEP READING AS I CLEAR THE AIR AND GIVE A CLEAR, SINCERE, AND DECISIVE TRUE PERSPECTIVE ON THIS MOST SENSITIVE AND VERY IMPORTANT MATTER CALLED **"POLICE-ENCOUNTERS."**

Black-Lives-Matter and other leading national Black organizations need to take a very close look at this chapter about obeying the Police as well. Because once they fully understand, they will recognize that most of these Black men are getting themselves injured or killed by not following the proper procedures, not using common sense, and not respecting the structure and law in our civilized society when they encounter the Police. --- THE TRUTH IS: MANY, OR MOST BLACKS, AND MANY WHITES ARE "VERY" MISLED IN THEIR UNDERSTANDING WHEN IT COMES TO THIS ISSUE OF "POLICE-ENCOUNTERS." MANY OF THESE PEOPLE DO NOT UNDERSTAND THE AUTHORITY OF THE POLICE OFFICER NOR THEIR RIGHTS AS A CITIZEN. MY AIM IN THIS SECTION IS TO CLEAR THE AIR ON THESE MISCONCEPTIONS AND MISLEAD THOUGHT PROCESSES. PLEASE ALLOW ME TO PROVE MY POINT. LET ME GET STARTED.

I cannot, with a clear conscience, complete this book without addressing what some so-called Black leaders and sympathizers deem to be Police brutality and wrongful Police actions against the Black Community. This chapter in this book is probably the most important because it actually deals with fundamental laws and principles that could actually lead to life or death situations and outcomes. There are so many people, White, Black, and others, who have a very misled and "grave" misunderstanding of the government, the Police, and what an individual citizen's rights are when it comes to police-encounters.

This gross misunderstanding on behalf of these misled citizens has led to many violent police-encounters, deaths, and many situations making citizens feel that they are being mistreated and/or brutalized by the Police. Many Black Citizens have a gross misguided fear about the Police. And on the reverse-side of these warped ideas psychologically embedded in the psyche of these Black citizens by unwarranted rhetoric; it has also put Police Officers in more of a defensive mode or posture and caused them to be more on high-alert, and further makes them feel less respected and safe. This creates a tense situation. Furthermore, it de-humanizes the Police. Therefore, under this negative stimulus, the Citizens and the Police have a more intensified encounter and situation. This creates a lose-lose situation for both sides and for our society as a whole.

This major gap in understanding and respect between the Police and these particular citizens leads to more violence, death, and disharmony in America. And those so-called leaders who do not understand police-encounters, or who intentionally fan the flames of this discord are further to blame. Some Blacks are so gullible that they believe everything they hear. Some Blacks are just too immature to have a clear understanding. Some Blacks just do not understand the role of government, and more specifically the role of the Police. And some are just down-right rebellious.

My sincere goal in this section of this book is to educate both sides on this issue, which if left unaddressed, leads to more anarchy and leads our society more astray.

MY AIM IS NOT TO SIDE WITH THE POLICE, NOR SIDE WITH THE CITIZENS. MY AIM IS TO TELL THE TRUTH, EXPLAIN THE LAW IN GENERAL, AND TO STAND ON THE SIDE OF JUSTICE AND FAIR-TREATMENT TO BRING MORE HARMONY, PEACE, AND BALANCE WITHIN OUR AMERICAN SOCIETY. I PERSONALLY CHOOSE TO BE PART OF THE SOLUTION; RATHER THAN A PART OF THE PROBLEM.

This chapter is just a GENERAL OVERVIEW of how our society works when it comes to our Police and police-encounters; in addition to how citizens are supposed to interact with the Police and the general laws and constitutional protections and rights on both sides. This is certainly not legal advice. Furthermore, this is not to speak on specific arrests, specific police-encounters, or specific deaths that have happened within certain police-encounters. I believe those are to be judged on a case-by-case basis according to the law. Which I believe is the aim of our criminal justice system in every case.

Also, which I am sad to say, I am sure there are Police Officers who may at times cross certain boundaries; or Police Officers who do not follow the law and rules as it applies to them on occasions; or some who may not follow the law none of the time (this one I find very hard to believe). I know there are some Police Officers who over-step their bounds from time-to-time and some who sometimes lose their temper in certain situations. This is not right. But, this is to be expected. No system is perfect, and no system can control the behavior of every single cop until they are caught in a violation. There are some bad cops out there. There are some cops that have short tempers and do not do the right thing. We also must recognize that we do not live in a perfect society, and thus, neither are the Police nor our police department's perfect. This section of the book is not to deal with those types of situations and issues. THIS SECTION IS DEALING WITH WHAT A CITIZEN IS SUPPOSE TO DO DURING THE POLICE-ENCOUNTER. Frankly and personally, I think that MOST Police Officers are out to do a fair days' work and try to abide by the rules and laws as much as they possibly can, White and Black.

We must remember that Police Officers are not all White today. Police Officers are White, Black, Asian, Mexican, Latino, and others. This further goes against those who always falsely claim White racism embedded in the police departments. Police Officers are also male and female today.

Now, I would like to once again offer my credentials as I write about this topic. Again, this is not legal advice, but rather a GENERAL overview of what should be expected from Police and what the general laws and rules are when citizens encounter the Police, and of course basic common sense.

I am qualified to write on this particular topic because I have a Juris Doctorate degree in Jurisprudence. Jurisprudence is the study of law. Furthermore, I have a Bachelor's degree in Political Science. These credentials and educational tools give me the background and the confidence to be able to address this topic with a certain amount of accuracy and educational practicality and expertise. And most importantly, I will combine my educational background in law and politics with the sheer common sense that we ALL possess to render a synopsis that will surely help both sides of this issue known as police-encounters.

Furthermore, as I have expressed earlier in this book, I firmly believe in the basic and fundamental principles of the Bible, which also tremendously helps to substantiate and confirm my points.

And lastly, I wish to say that, for many, most of this information is very simple and straight forward, and many already know it. However, there seems to be many people, especially in the Black community, who do not understand these concepts and/or have been misled by listening and believing the rhetoric that is untrue. And maybe some are just downright rebellious. Nevertheless, the information provided is for those blacks and others who do not quite understand; but who wish to understand.

Again, it must be said, we all have to follow the law or we will not have a civilized society. I do not want to live in a society that does not have rules and laws to follow. It would be chaotic, there would be anarchy, and a jungle with no guarantee of an individual's survival. Let it be known that laws create a system of fairness, peace, and harmony. At least, that is supposed to be the aim. And here, I sincerely believe that this is the goal of America.

Again, America is the greatest nation in the world to live in and we are favored by GOD. Why? Because America has the greatest ever-evolving collection of well thought out fair Rules, fair Laws, and a fair Constitution; which all stem directly from Biblical principles that aim to make America a great environment and a great country for mankind to live within, in harmony and peace. This is why America is blessed by the almighty GOD and by the Universe. We strive through our laws to render fair-play and justice through Biblical principles. That is what America is about ultimately; the rules, the laws, and the fair-play we try to live by stemming from biblical principles. America has a great body of laws. **WE ARE A NATION OF LAWS.** As I have stated before, go to other countries and see what kind of rules and laws they have and see how you are treated there. I am sure you will be back very soon.

A society that lives in a civilized capacity must have those people or citizens (the government) who enforce the rules and laws if we want peace and harmony to abound. And thus, we need Police Officers (Government employees). Really, in many respects, the law enforcement systems make boys become men. It makes girls become women. It makes irresponsible teenagers become responsible adults. It teaches people how to be responsible and follow the law. If it were not for Police Officers many young men and young women would not have evolved into the great men or women they are today. If a person is not corrected when they break the law, they may think it is okay and continue to do it. At that point, we would have a chaotic and lawless society ruled by Satan; a society that would not survive.

Of course the law has to be applied appropriately to everyone. The law has to be neutrally applied to everyone the same. I know some Blacks may say, well the law is not applied equally to everyone.

WELL, I WOULD SAY TO THOSE BLACKS, FIRST, PLEASE MAKE SURE YOU ARE FOLLOWING THE LAW YOURSELF.

ONLY THEN CAN ONE COMPLAIN IF THEY THEMSELVES ARE DOING WHAT THEY ARE SUPPOSE TO DO. AND AT THAT POINT, IF YOU CAN, SUE THE PERPETRATOR IN CIVIL COURT, OR PRESS CRIMINAL CHARGES IF YOU FEEL YOU HAVE BEEN WRONGED. In other words, sue the Police Officer in civil court or file criminal charges if you can and have a viable claim. We do have remedies in America for such behaviors. Get paid for their mistakes the right way. Furthermore, one cannot control someone else's behavior; one can only react to it. So again, sue them, if you can. There is always a right way in America.

Having rules and laws that we all must follow is just common sense to me. But, for those who it may help to have a biblical reference as well:

> **In the Bible's New Testament, the first part of Romans chapter 13 verse 1 clearly states "Obey the government, for GOD is the one that put it there." And further Romans chapter 13 verse 2 states, "So those who refuse to obey the laws of the land are refusing to obey GOD, and punishment will follow." Also, in the Old Testament in Exodus chapter 22 verse 28 it says "You shall not blaspheme GOD, nor curse government officials---your judges and your rulers."**

So therefore, according to scriptures of the Bible, everybody, Black and White, and all those in-between, are suppose to follow and respect the law of the land, and more specifically in America because that is where we live; or in the alternative suffer the consequences of your own actions. But, moreso, the ultimate consequences of GOD. We all must respect and follow the direction of Police Officers when confronted with those types of situations. Again, it does not matter if you are Black, White, Brown, Yellow, Red, Green, Purple or Blue; everyone is subject to the rules and the laws.

If you are the type of Person that does not think you have to respect and honor the Police, then you will probably not like the following writings in this book. However, I am not overly concerned if you happen to not like the writings in this book, because really, this chapter in this book serves to educate ALL people on the do's and don'ts when encountering Police Officers. That's it.

I REPEAT: THIS BOOK PRIMARILY DEALS WITH THE POLICE-ENCOUNTER ITSELF, NOT NECESSARILY ANY OF THE AFTERMATHS.

AGAIN, THE SAD NEWS IS THIS: BASICALLY, SATAN IS CONVINCING MANY BLACK PEOPLE TO BELIEVE LIES AND FALSE RHETORIC, WHICH IS CAUSING MANY BLACK PEOPLE TO GET THEMSELVES HARMED OR KILLED WITHIN POLICE ENCOUNTERS.

THIS BOOK AIMS TO DESTROY AN EVIL BLACK PSYCHOLOGICAL PSYCHOSIS ABOUT POLICE-ENCOUNTERS, AND SOME BLACK PEOPLE'S FALSE CLAIMS OF RACISM. THIS BOOK IS THE CURE!

These writings will probably save someone's life and are aimed directly at creating more harmony between American Citizens and the Police. Nevertheless, allow me to continue to address this all too familiar cry from some of the Black community about so-called Police brutality, so-called over-kill, and so-called Police misconduct.

Again, this should not be considered legal advice. Every police-encounter has its own unique characteristics and circumstances; which requires a unique application of the law under those particular unique characteristics and circumstances. Furthermore, I will probably not address any "particular" or "specific" police-encounter, any particular case of alleged Police brutality, any particular case of excessive force, or any particular case of unnecessary use of deadly force. This will continue to be just a general overview of what police-encounters should entail, without reference to any specific or particular case or situation.

Nevertheless, the first thing Blacks and others need to know is that Police Officers have AUTHORITY granted to them by the states that allows them to enforce the law and to investigate any potential violations of the law. Police Officers are UNEQUIVOCALLY granted this right.

I have heard some celebrities and others say that the Police Officer is the servant to the public. That is not totally true. The Police Officer is a servant to the public only to keep law-and-order and possibly to serve the public within their own Police discretion if the public needs assistance to prevent them from harm or from a criminal act.

THE POLICE ARE NOT YOUR OR MY PERSONAL PUBLIC SERVANTS!

Let's get this straight right now! The Police Officer is a servant to the GENERAL PUBLIC to keep and enforce law-and-order; not our personal public servant to serve us personally! His job is to serve the public to keep law-and-order when necessary. So, when a Police Officer stops or detains you and/or questions you and he has a "reasonable suspicion" or "probable cause," the Police Officer does in-fact have the authority to investigate you and the situation to determine if there is a criminal issue or law violated.

Furthermore, being detained or stopped is not being arrested. Being detained is only to give the Officer a reasonable amount time to investigate the situation and you based on the fact that he is "reasonably suspicious" that there is a violation of the law, or that a crime has been, is being, or is about to be committed. "Reasonable suspicion" basically means that the Officer has reasonable objectively justifiable specific and articulable facts and/or circumstances that some type of violation of law has been committed, or that a crime has been, is being, or is about to be committed.

At minimum, an Officer "only" has to have "reasonable suspicion" to stop and/or to detain you and to investigate the situation and you. "Reasonable suspicion" could simply mean that someone fits a description of a criminal suspect; or a suspect who drops a suspicious object after seeing police; or a suspect in a high crime area who runs after seeing Police; or a suspect acting nervous and answering questions inconsistently; and for many other justifiable reasons. However, "reasonable suspicion" may not apply if a person simply refuses to answer questions or is of a certain ethnicity or race.

Being detained is usually called a Terry Stop. A Terry Stop generally can last up to 20 minutes while the Police Officer investigates you and/or the situation. Also, once you are detained for "reasonable suspicion," even though you are not under arrest, an officer is allowed to pat you down to check for weapons for his own personal safety, and yours.

During that detainment and investigation for "reasonable suspicion," if the Officer reaches the threshold of "probable cause" that a violation of law has occurred, or that a crime has been, is being, or is about to be committed, then, at that point he may take further appropriate actions and/or arrest you; or the Officer may write you a ticket as the law dictates or do as he sees fit within some discretion.

"Probable cause" means that the Officer is basically 50 percent or more certain that a violation of the law, or that a crime has been, is being, or is about to be committed. If the Officer does not reach the threshold of "probable cause" during the detainment and investigation within a reasonable amount of time, at that point you are probably free to go. But, if the Officer does not release you on his own at that point, then, you should or may simply ask courteously "Officer, am I free to go?" And if he says yes, then go. If he says no, then politely allow him to finish his investigation because you are still being detained.

MORE SPECIFICALLY: Generally, a Police Officer can certainly stop and detain you if the Police Officer has "reasonable suspicion" of a violation of law; or "reasonable suspicion" that a crime has been, is being, or is about to be committed; or if the Officer has "probable cause" of a violation of law he may detain you and take further appropriate actions and/or arrest you if the law so dictates; or if he has "probable cause" of a crime that has been, is being, or is about to be committed the Officer may detain and/or arrest you if the law so dictates; if the Officer has seen you violate certain laws he may detain, ticket, and/or arrest you; an Officer may stop and detain you if he has seen or suspects a traffic violation; the traffic violation can be as minor as your license plate bulb being out, or a tail light bulb being out, or you not coming to a complete stop at a stop sign or stop light, and in his discretion he may also write you a ticket; an Officer may detain you if he has been called by a citizen or anyone stating that a possible law has been violated, and/or a crime has been, is being, or is about to be committed by you; and an Officer may take action if someone is in danger, and/or if there are exigent or dangerous circumstances where they need to protect someone and/or the public; and/or if they have a search warrant and/or an arrest warrant. Any of the above reasons are legitimate and legal reasons that allow a Police Officer the authority to get involved.

Their job is to protect and serve the general public from crime and harm and to enforce the laws of their particular state in America. IF YOU DO NOT WANT TO HAVE ENCOUNTERS WITH THE POLICE OR DO NOT WANT TO BE STOPPED BY POLICE, DO NOT DO ANYTHING THAT CREATES "REASONABLE SUSPICION," "PROBABLE CAUSE," OR BREAK ANY LAW, AND YOU WILL PROBABLY NOT HAVE ANY PROBLEMS NOR HAVE TO DEAL WITH POLICE-ENCOUNTERS.

Therefore, a citizen who encounters the Police under these types of situations and other similar situations "<u>MUST</u>" and "<u>SHOULD</u>" comply with the Officers inquiries if he or she wants to be in compliance with what our US constitution and other laws support. Not doing so leads to situations that can go badly for you, and everybody. The Police Officer has a job to do and he or she has sworn under oath to do it. And furthermore, he or she has received training on what the law allows him or her to do, and not to do. It is no big deal; **SO JUST RELAX AND COOPERATE.**

Also, if you are detained in your vehicle by the Police turn your music off so you guys can communicate clearly; keep your hands visible so the Officer can see them or put them where he tells you to put them; and put all of your windows down so the Officer can clearly see inside your vehicle for his safety and yours, especially tinted windows; unless he says otherwise; and do not make any sudden moves. In other words, comply with the Officer as much as possible.

Not allowing the Police Officer to do his or her job by not allowing them to complete his or her investigation is a violation of the law within itself. It is called "obstruction-of-justice." This means that you are impeding or interfering with the Officers investigation or you are not allowing the Officer to fulfill his sworn duties as a Police Officer while he is on the scene. This can be perpetrated intentionally or unintentionally by the perpetrator who is being investigated, or by a bystander.

And therefore, at that point, the perpetrator is definitely in violation of the law and can be subject to whatever penalties may apply, more-than-likely even arrest. **SO JUST RELAX AND COOPERATE.**

Also, just to make it clear, even if you are a general bystander, a husband, a wife, a boyfriend, a girlfriend, a relative or friend, or anybody that is interfering with the Police Officer's investigation of that person or situation, you can be arrested and charged with "obstruction-of-justice;" as well as becoming a suspect of the potential crime or violation of law. I see people standing around many times with their cell phones out video recording and shouting at the Police and trying to interfere with the Police Officers job or investigation. Well, that may be okay and a good thing to keep Cops accountable, if done from a distance and it does not impede or hinder the investigation.

However, please remember, when you do that, if the Officer tells you to get back or stay away, you must comply. If you do not, you are subject to arrest for "obstruction of his investigation;" and I have seen people get arrested for this many times.

JUST TO REITERATE: A BYSTANDER CANNOT IMPEDE, DISTURB, OR BLOCK AN OFFICERS INVESTIGATION, AND IF YOU DO, YOU CAN AND PROBABLY WILL BE ARRESTED FOR "OBSTRUCTION-OF-JUSTICE."

IF YOU ARE A BYSTANDER IN ANY CAPACITY, PLEASE REMEMBER THIS, THE OFFICER DOES NOT KNOW WHO YOU ARE; HE DOES NOT KNOW WHAT YOUR MOTIVES ARE; HE DOES NOT KNOW IF YOU ARE ARMED WITH A WEAPON OR NOT; HE DOES NOT KNOW IF YOU WILL HARM OR INJURE HIM; AND HE DOES NOT KNOW WHAT YOU WILL DO IF HE HAPPENS TO TURN HIS BACK TO YOU. PLEASE, PUT YOURSELF IN HIS SHOES. WHAT WOULD YOU DO?

EMPATHY:

IT IS VERY IMPORTANT TO BE ABLE TO "EMPATHIZE" WITH THE POLICE OFFICER. Put yourself in the Police Officer's shoes. How would you feel if you were a Police Officer under some of these same circumstances that they confront daily? I am sure you would understand better if you put yourself in their shoes. So please, show the same common courtesy and respect for Police Officer's that you yourself would expect. In most cases, they are only trying to do their job. And remember, there is a whole lot of fake-news and false stories out here when it comes police-encounters.

THE OFFICER MUST SECURE HIS SAFETY FIRST AND FOREMOST ONCE HE IS ON A SCENE BY ANY MEANS HE OR SHE CAN TO COMPLETE HIS OR HER INVESTIGATION. This is why they usually call for back-up. It is rather silly to be holding a cell phone recording the Police and yelling and/or cursing at them while they are doing a legitimate investigation; especially if you are too close. So do not be surprised when or if you are pulled into the investigation and arrested for obstruction of a police investigation, because they certainly have the discretion to do it if you are too close and/or you are having an impact on the situation or investigation.

Now, back to the one-on-one police-encounter; not following the Officer's request only exacerbates the situation for the worst. It also creates tension and puts everyone on the defensive, which puts everyone in jeopardy of violence and/or in harm's way. A Police Officer must also take control of the situation when he encounters a citizen to protect his own safety. **REMEMBER, GENERALLY, HE DOES NOT KNOW WHO YOU ARE.** And there are killers and criminals out there that are trying to evade Police, harm the Police, and/or harm the general public, and you could be one of them, the Police do not always know.

FURTHERMORE, EVEN IF HE DOES KNOW WHO YOU ARE, HE CANNOT BE CERTAIN THAT YOU WILL NOT HARM HIM AT ANY GIVEN MOMENT. YOU COULD BE HAVING A VERY BAD DAY. So, from the very start, a Police Officer has to be very careful to secure his or her own safety during a stop, or during an investigation. This is why they are equipped with the tools that they have. There are many violent and crazy people in the world. -----So, if you are one of those people who challenges his authority and will not cooperate, you are certainly creating a situation that can escalate and have serious consequences and put you and the Officer in danger of bodily harm. You are WRONG for doing this. Please cooperate Black people (or any people for that matter). In other words, the ABSOLUTE right thing to do is to fully cooperate and let the Police Officer do his or her job as he or she is sworn to do and has the authority to do.

When the Police Officer stops you for any of the above legitimate reasons or in any of the above situations, he has complete authority by the state to investigate the situation to his satisfaction, and OUR job is to fully cooperate and make that investigation go as smoothly as possible.

Normally, if you cooperate, things go much smoother, and normally the Officer will cut you as much of a break as he can. In most cases, Police Officers have this kind of flexibility and discretion. Discretion, meaning, that if the Police Officer wants to cut you a break, or not enforce the law to the maximum extent, he has the flexibility or discretion to do so. But, why would he do that if you are not cooperating and you are giving him a hard time? Remember, he can cut you a break, but he is not necessarily required to. It is basically his choice. So please respect it. Furthermore, being cooperative makes things go quicker, there is less tension, and after the Officer is satisfied with the results of his investigation, you can be on your merry-way, if the situation dictates that. **SO JUST RELAX AND COOPERATE.**

It is quite repugnant to see Citizens act as though they are above the law; and/or acting as though a Police Officer has no authority; and/or just being unnecessarily disrespectful or uncooperative.

For instance, in Texas, driving without your safety belt on is against the law. So, if I choose to drive my vehicle without my seatbelt on and the Police stop me for that reason, then I have brought this police-encounter upon myself because I have violated Texas law. Therefore, I should not be angry or mad with the Police Officer for doing his job by stopping me for not wearing my seatbelt. Furthermore, if I choose to be uncooperative and disrespectful towards the Police during the legitimate police-encounter, he may begin to look for other laws that I have broken while I am detained, which could make things more difficult for me.

So, my point again is why not accept your responsibilities when you have violated the law and respect the Police Officer as you know you should, or as we know we should.

Also, again, the Officer has to be very careful to protect his safety from physical harm. I cannot overstate this fact. And again, in most cases, the officer does not know you, and thus does not know what you are capable of doing. So for the Officer, it is already a tense situation which does not help. When encountering you, the Officer must secure his safety first and foremost. Again, he would not be there if he was not called, or if he did not have "reasonable suspicion" of a crime, or if he did not have "probable cause" of a crime being committed or that has been committed, or if he had not observed a crime being committed, or if he did not have an arrest or search warrant, or for some other legitimate legal reason stated above.

So, therefore, AGAIN, he has a right and a duty to be there to enforce the law, and the law only. You must follow all of the Officer's directions or in most cases, if you do not, you are putting yourself in legal jeopardy or in harms-way and things will not or may not go as well for you. And you may just get yourself injured or killed.

SO AGAIN, TO SET THE RECORD STRAIGHT, THE FIRST THING YOU NEED TO KNOW IS THAT YOU ARE OBLIGATED AND MUST COMPLY BECAUSE THE POLICE OFFICER DOES HAVE THE AUTHORITY TO RECTIFY THE SITUATION IF HE IS THERE FOR A LEGITIMATE REASON AS STATED ABOVE. THE POLICE OFFICER IS NOT YOUR PERSONAL PUBLIC SERVANT; HE IS A SERVANT OF THE GENERAL PUBLIC TO ENFORCE THE LAW AND TO FOSTER LAW-AND-ORDER.

FURTHERMORE, EXERCISING A LITTLE COMMON SENSE GOES A LONG WAY. REMEMBER, HE IS ONLY THERE TO DO HIS JOB. A POLICE OFFICER IS HUMAN TOO. WHY BE NASTY AND DISRESPECTFUL? IT IS JUST UNNECESSARY AND IT MAKES THE SITUATION THAT MUCH MORE INTENSE. A POLICE OFFICER IS NOT PERFECT. HOWEVER, GUESS WHAT, NEITHER ARE YOU OR I. NOT ONE OF US IS INFALLIBLE.

So, when a person, any person, whether they be black, white, green, purple, or blue, does not comply with a Police Officer it is most likely a violation and that puts the Officer on high-alert and it intensifies the situation for the worst. If you make any strange moves, the Officer may see it as a physical threat or aggression against him. He just might react with deadly force and harm you.

He could also possibly react and harm you by accident.

A Police Officer must be aware of all movements and actions made by citizens. REMEMBER, AGAIN, HE DOES NOT KNOW YOU NOR WHAT CRIME YOU MAY HAVE COMMITTED -- MURDER, ASSAULT, AND/OR YOU MAY HAVE A DEADLY WEAPON ETC. Furthermore, if you are not cooperating, it puts him more on edge creating a more dangerous situation for you and possibly for him. This is how more accidents happen.

WHEN POLICE OFFICERS HAVE BEEN HARMED OR KILLED IN THE PAST, IT HAS HAPPENED IN A SPLIT-SECOND. IT HAPPENS QUICKLY, AND THEREFORE POLICE MUST ACT OR REACT QUICKLY WHEN THEY ARE ON THE JOB. THESE ARE SPLIT-SECOND DECISIONS AND REACTIONS THEY ARE REQUIRED TO MAKE. THEIR LIVES ARE ON THE LINE AT ALL TIMES. And in their training, Police Officers have seen other fellow officers on film get killed in split-seconds. This puts Officers on an even greater high-alert and creates more intensity and tension, which again creates more potential for deadly reactions and mistakes.

REMEMBER, MISTAKES CAN HAPPEN, AND MORE MISTAKES **"DO"** HAPPEN WHEN THERE IS TENSION AND INTENSITY CREATED ON YOUR BEHALF, OR ON ANYONE'S BEHALF. ALSO, WHEN ADRENALINE IS FLOWING, THERE IS MORE POTENTIAL FOR ACCIDENTS, MISUNDERSTANDINGS, AND MISHAPS. THIS IS EXACTLY WHAT HAS HAPPENED TO MANY BLACKS WHO HAVE BEEN SHOT, INJURED, AND/OR KILLED BY POLICE OFFICERS.

FURTHERMORE, YOU SHOULD NEVER RESIST A POLICE OFFICER IN ANY MANNER IF THEY ARE THERE FOR ANY OF THE FORE-STATED LEGITIMATE REASONS ABOVE. RESISTING ARREST IS ANOTHER SEPARATE VERY SERIOUS OFFENSE. If a Police Officer gives you orders to do something, and he has the right to be there, you should absolutely do it. Otherwise, suffer the consequences of your own actions if you put yourself in harm's way. And please, you should not be complaining when you are injured, or when things turn out badly for you because it could be because of your own actions. So please, protect yourself by doing the right thing and following the Police Officer's orders, if at all possible.

Anytime you resist a Police Officer, or resist arrest, under the situations stated above, you potentially are in violation of the law and further you are putting yourself in harm's way. And assaulting an Officer is certainly a MAJOR offense and is never the right thing to do. Assaulting a Police Officer can possibly get you up to 15 years under many legal scenarios. And certainly, killing a Police Officer is a capital felony, punishable by the death penalty or life imprisonment without the possibility of release under many laws. So you certainly do not want to be guilty of that.

AGAIN, they are only doing the job that they are sworn to do. Furthermore, they are just trying to go home safely to their family at the end of the day after giving a fair days work. What's wrong with giving Police Officers respect and allowing them to fulfill their job responsibilities? Nothing! Again, noncooperation can lead to unwanted results. SO JUST RELAX AND COOPERATE.

THEREFORE AGAIN, ALLOW ME TO GIVE YOU THE BASIC GIST OF THIS BOOK!

AGAIN, IF YOU DO NOT WANT TO BE INJURED NOR KILLED BY POLICE DURING A POLICE-ENCOUNTER, PLEASE REMEMBER THIS, AND HERE THE FOLLOWING CLEARLY:

ONCE A POLICE OFFICER HAS ARRIVED ON A SCENE WITH DUE AUTHORITY, AS EXPRESSED ABOVE, AT THAT POINT, TECHNICALLY YOU ARE NO LONGER FREE TO DO AS YOU PLEASE FOR THAT TIME PERIOD. FROM THAT MOMENT FORWARD, YOU ARE NOT YOUR OWN, YOU ARE NOT FREE TO DO ANYTHING AS YOU PLEASE, YOU BELONG TO, AND ARE A PART OF THE POLICE OFFICER'S INVESTIGATION. YOU THEREFORE MUST, AND SHOULD, AT THAT POINT, FOR THE DURATION OF HIS OR HER INVESTIGATION, OBEY ALL THE OFFICERS' REQUEST AND DEMANDS. KEEP YOUR HANDS WHERE THE OFFICER CAN SEE THEM, PREFERREBLY ON THE STEERING WHEEL, OR WHERE EVER HE TELLS YOU TO PUT THEM. IF HE CANNOT SEE CLEARLY INTO YOUR VEHICLE, PUT ALL OF YOUR WINDOWS DOWN. DO NOT MAKE ANY SUDDEN MOVES. DO NOT BE UNCOOPERATIVE. TRY TO ANSWER ALL THE

OFFICERS' QUESTIONS, IF POSSIBLE. THIS IS OUR DUTY AS A CITIZEN BECAUSE FOR THE DURATION OF YOUR POLICE-ENCOUNTER, BASICALLY, THE OFFICER IS GENERALLY IN CHARGE AND IN CONTROL. THE OFFICER IS TRAINED TO TAKE TOTAL CONTROL OF THE POLICE-ENCOUNTER AND POLICE INVESTIGATION. ALSO, YOU SHOULD NOT BE VIDEO RECORDING THE POLICE-ENCOUNTER, ESPECIALLY IF THE OFFICER TELLS YOU TO PUT YOUR RECORDING DEVICE AWAY. THE OFFICER COULD TELL YOU THIS FOR THE SAFETY OF THE SITUATION, TO EXPEDITE OR NOT TO IMPEDE THE INVESTIGATION, OR FOR ANY OTHER REASON.

AND AGAIN, FOR YOU BYSTANDERS: JUST TO MAKE IT CLEAR, EVEN IF YOU ARE A GENERAL BYSTANDER, A HUSBAND, A WIFE, A BOYFRIEND, A GIRLFRIEND, A RELATIVE OR FRIEND, OR ANYBODY THAT IS INTERFERING OR DISRUPTING THE POLICE OFFICER'S INVESTIGATION OF THAT PERSON OR SITUATION, YOU CAN BE ARRESTED AND CHARGED WITH "OBSTRUCTION-OF-JUSTICE;" AS WELL AS POSSIBLY BECOMING A SUSPECT OF THE POTENTIAL CRIME OR VIOLATION OF LAW.

AND THUS, WE AS BLACK PEOPLE, CAN NEVER CLAIM "POLICE BRUTALITY" IF WE ARE NOT DOING OUR PART AND COOPERATING AS A CITIZEN SHOULD DO DURING THE POLICE-ENCOUNTER. SO AGAIN, JUST RELAX AND COOPERATE.

ALSO AGAIN, JUST FOR THE RECORD: THERE IS "NO" MASS CONSPIRACY (LOCAL, STATE, OR NATIONAL) BY POLICE OFFICERS OR BY POLICE DEPARTMENTS TO INJURE OR KILL BLACK PEOPLE!

POLICE ARE AN ABSOLUTELY ESSENTIAL, INDISPENSABLE, AND NECESSARY COMPONENT OF OUR AMERICAN SOCIETY; AND WE CANNOT THRIVE AND/OR SURVIVE WITHOUT THEM.

Now, I am aware that some of this may not sound fair. I am aware that some may not want to hear this. But, I am only telling you what the law says. The law applies to all of us the same; at least it is suppose to. I have seen Black men fighting against Police Officers and not cooperating, and when they are shot and/or injured, they want to claim Police brutality, Police misconduct, and/or racism. Well, don't be a liar. Please cooperate with the Police and you will not have to worry about such things.

Are there times when Police Officers make mistakes? Yes, of course. Are there some hot-headed Cops out there that lose their tempers sometimes? Yes, probably. Do Police Officers have bad days sometimes and are more aggressive than normal because of it? Yes, probably. Are there times when Police Officers allow their personal life to affect their duties? Yes, probably. Are there times when Police Officers over-step there bounds and authority? Yes, probably. Will there be times when citizens are right and the Police Officer is wrong? Yes, probably. But, fight that fight in a court of law in front of a judge AFTER the police-encounter and investigation; if necessary. Generally, the odds are too great against you during the police-encounter and investigation because the Officer has more authority than you at that particular time. Again, it is best to fight against the Police in court rather than during the police-encounter. Better yet, do not break the law at all, and you should not have these problems.

Are all Police Officers racist against Black men and Black people? Absolutely not. Are they targeting Blacks to kill and commit genocide against the Black race? Absolutely not. Police Officers are only trying to do their job and go home safely after a hard or fair days' work just like everyone else.

Nevertheless, Police Officers just happen to have a more inherently and more potentially dangerous job with greater risk of bodily harm and death, than others. And their job is probably more stressful. Therefore, we must and should respect and honor their services.

Also, remember, as I stated before, Police Officers are Black, White, Latino, Asian, and all other races now. They are also female. So Black people quit trying to deflect and act as though Police Officers are all White and are racist against Blacks. Or that the law-enforcement system is set up against Blacks to physically harm us. We have Blacks on the boards and in the legislative process participating in making laws for Police as well. Each situation should be analyzed on a case-by-case basis, as they have been.

So, when you do not cooperate with the Police Officer, remember you are putting yourself in harm's way. So please do not start crying and lying when things do not turn out in your favor. Be a big enough man or woman to accept those consequences. **WE ARE NOT BABIES OR CHILDREN! BLACKS ARE NOT ABOVE THE LAW! NO ONE IS ABOVE THE LAW!** And you do have a responsibility to obey the law and to cooperate with Police Officers just like everyone else, or suffer the consequences. That goes for all of us.

Furthermore, and to be quite honest, if I were a Police Officer, and I had a choice of my safety or the criminal's, and I was aware that the criminal was trying to shoot or cause serious bodily harm against me, and I am within my legal authority to take action against the criminal at that time, believe me, I would not hesitate to protect myself first and foremost; just like anyone else would or should do. In other words, yes, I would shoot the suspect without question, if I knew he was trying to seriously harm, kill, or shoot me. That is really just basic self-defense.

THERE ARE TOO MANY BLACK PEOPLE OUT HERE MAKING EXCUSES FOR NOT DOING THE RIGHT THING BY FOLLOWING POLICE OFFICERS COMMANDS. THERE ARE TOO MANY BLACK PEOPLE OUT THERE WHO BREAK THE LAW AND THEN DO NOT WANT TO MAN-UP OR WOMAN-UP WHEN FACED WITH THE LEGITIMATE LEGAL CONSEQUENCES. PLEASE! I HAVE NEITHER SYMPATHY NOR EMPATHY FOR PEOPLE WHO FIGHT AGAINST LAW-AND-ORDER AND THEN DO NOT WANT TO FACE THE LEGAL CONSEQUENCES! IT DOES NOT MAKE SENSE TO ME.

Also, many Blacks tell lies and put false spins on what really happened during their police-encounter. They have the Black community and others believing that the Police Officers are being brutal, when in reality, generally, the Police Officer is justified in the actions that they have taken. AND FURTHERMORE, WHEN THE OFFICER IS RIGHTFULLY ACQUITTED BY THE GRAND JURY OR JURY, THE BLACK COMMUNITY AND SOMETIMES OTHERS WRONGFULLY THINK THAT THE POLICE OFFICERS ARE GETTING AWAY WITH WRONG-DOING AND ARE NOT BEING HELD ACCOUNTABLE, WHICH IS SO UNTRUE. This is an ongoing very sick cycle and Blacks need to stop creating these lies and falsehoods and tell the truth.

THE TRUTH IS: THERE IS "NO" MASS CONSPIRACY (LOCAL, STATE, OR NATIONAL) BY POLICE OFFICERS OR BY POLICE DEPARTMENTS TO INJURE OR KILL BLACK PEOPLE!

As stated before several times, Black people in most cases are getting themselves harmed or killed by not cooperating with Police Officers.

SOMEONE NEEDS TO CONTINUE TO TELL BLACK PEOPLE THE TRUTH, LIKE I AM DOING, AND THAT IS: YOU ARE GETTING YOURSELVES INJURED OR KILLED BY NOT COOPERATING WITH THE POLICE, AND BY ACTING AS THOUGH YOU ARE ABOVE THE LAW. THEN SOME OF YOU LIE TO THE GENERAL PUBLIC ABOUT WHAT REALLY TOOK PLACE IN MANY CASES. STOP IT!

I understand you may not have known the law in the past, or thought that what you were doing was okay, or thought you were right in an encounter with a Police Officer. BUT, NOW YOU KNOW WHAT TO DO, AND THUS THERE IS NO EXCUSE. IF YOU ARE INJURED OR KILLED, IT IS PROBABLY YOUR FAULT. AND ALSO REMEMBER, MORE MISTAKES ARE MADE WHEN TENSION IS CREATED. AND IT IS NOT TOO SMART TO CREATE TENSION WITH SOMEONE ELSE WHO HAS A GUN AND THE LEGAL AUTHORITY TO USE IT, AND YOU DO NOT HAVE ONE. THAT IS NOT SMART AT ALL. AND YOU MUST ALSO REMEMBER, AS A BLACK MAN OR WOMAN, TYPICALLY WE ARE BIGGER AND STRONGER THAN THE AVERAGE WHITE, MEXICAN, OR, ASIAN PERSON. ALSO, BLACK YOUTH SOMETIMES LOOK LIKE ADULTS TO SOME POLICE OFFICERS THAT ARE NOT PART OF OUR RACE. AND SOME OF THEM DO NOT UNDERSTAND OUR CULTURE AT ALL.

AND I AM ONLY STATING THE ABOVE TO GET US TO SEE WHAT SOME OF THE POSSIBLE THOUGHTS COULD BE IN THE MIND OF AN OFFICER DURING A POLICE-ENCOUNTER. IF A POLICE OFFICER PERCIEVES SOMEONE AS BIGGER AND STRONGER, HE OR SHE MIGHT BE JUSTIFIED IN PERCIEVING THAT PERSON AS A THREAT OF DEATH IF YOU ARE FIGHTING THEM, AS OPPOSED TO SOMEONE SMALLER, BECAUSE THAT IS THE OFFICER'S HONEST PERCEPTION DURING THE POLICE-ENCOUNTER. IF YOU ARE A JUVENILE OR YOUNGSTER, BUT THE POLICE OFFICER PERCIEVES YOU AS AN ADULT, HIS OR HER ACTIONS MAY BE JUSTIFIED TOWARDS YOU EVEN THOUGH YOU ARE A JUVENILE OR YOUNGSTER BECAUSE THAT IS HIS OR HER HONEST PERCEPTION DURING THAT POLICE-ENCOUNTER. MUCH OF THE SCRUTINY IS REALLY ALL ABOUT WHAT THE POLICE OFFICER HONESTLY PERCEIVES, AND/OR BELIEVES, DURING THE PARTICULAR POLICE-ENCOUNTER, NOT THE AFTERMATH.

FURTHERMORE, AS I HAVE STATED BEFORE, IN POLICE-TRAINING, OFFICERS HAVE SEEN ON FILM OTHER COPS BEING SERIOUSLY INJURED OR KILLED BY BAD PEOPLE IN SPLIT-SECOND SCENARIOS. THIS FURTHER PUTS COPS ON EDGE. THE PSYCHE OF A POLICE OFFICER IS MUCH DIFFERENT FROM OUR PSYCHE AS CITIZENS BECAUSE OF THEIR POLICE-TRAINING AND THE FILMS THAT THEY HAVE WITNESSED OF OTHER COPS BEING SERIOUSLY INJURED OR KILLED ON DUTY BY BAD GUYS IN A SPLIT-SECOND BECAUSE THE COP MADE A MINOR

MISTAKE. SO THEY MUST TAKE EVERY PRECAUTION. AND THEY DO TAKE EVERY PRECAUTION. LIKE I SAID BEFORE, THEY DO NOT KNOW WHO YOU ARE NOR WHAT VIOLENCE YOU ARE CAPABLE OF.

AND FURTHERMORE, ONCE POLICE BEGAN SHOOTING AT A SUSPECT, ALL POLICE OFFICERS ARE TRAINED TO CONTINUE SHOOTING UNTIL THE THREAT IS STOPPED. THEY ARE NOT TRAINED TO SHOOT IN THE LEG OR TO WOUND.

POLICE ARE TAUGHT TO SHOOT OR TO USE LETHAL FORCE AS A LAST RESORT, AND ONLY WHEN THERE IS AN IMMEDIATE DEADLY THREAT OF SOMEONE'S LIFE, OR FOR THEIR OWN LIFE. THEY ARE TAUGHT TO SHOOT TO STOP THE THREAT. THEY ARE NOT TAUGHT TO SHOOT TO WOUND OR TO JUST INCAPACITATE. THEY ARE TAUGHT TO SHOOT AT THE BIGGEST TARGET ON

THE BODY WHICH IS CALLED THE CENTER OF MASS. THIS IS BASICALLY THE CHEST AREA. THEY ARE NOT TRAINED TO SHOOT TO WOUND SUCH AS IN THE ARM, LEG, FOOT, OR HAND BECAUSE THESE ARE SMALLER MORE DIFFICULT TARGETS TO HIT; AND HITTING THESE TARGETS STILL MAY NOT STOP THE THREAT.

ALSO, IF THEY <u>MISS</u> A SMALL OBJECT SUCH AS THE LEG, ARM, FOOT, OR HAND IT IS POSSIBLE A STRAY BULLET MAY HIT AN INNOCENT VICTIM. FURTHERMORE, THE BULLET COULD STILL GO <u>THROUGH</u> ONE OF THESE SMALLER BODY PARTS AND HIT AN INNOCENT VICTIM.

ALSO, POLICE ARE NOT TRAINED TO SHOOT IN THE HEAD BECAUSE IT IS A SMALLER MORE DIFFICULT TARGET AS WELL. I AM ONLY STATING WHAT THE CURRENT POLICE TRAINING GENERALLY ENTAILS. BELIEVE ME, I AM NOT TRYING TO JUSTIFY ANY WRONG-DOING, I AM JUST TRYING TO SHOW BLACK PEOPLE AND OTHERS WHAT ALL CAN BE IN THE MIND OF A COP WHEN THEY ENCOUNTER YOU.

AND THUS, THERE IS NO HUMANE WAY TO SHOOT A PERSON. POLICE WORK IS DIRTY WORK SOMETIMES; AND AT TIMES THAT WORK ENTAILS ENDING ONE PERSONS LIFE TO SAVE ANOTHER, AND/OR TO SAVE OTHER LIVES.

MAYBE COPS SHOULD BE TRAINED TO SHOOT IN THE LEG IN SOME CASES. HOWEVER, THAT IS SOMETHING THAT MUST BE APPROVED THROUGH OUR LEGISLATIVE

SYSTEMS. THAT IS WHY BLACKS AND OTHER CITIZENS SHOULD BE INVOLVED IN THE LEGISLATIVE PROCESS IF YOU FEEL THINGS SHOULD CHANGE. MAYBE COPS SHOULD BE RETRAINED. I DON'T KNOW. I AM NOT HERE TO MAKE THAT ARGUMENT. <u>AGAIN, I AM ONLY STATING THE CURRENT LAW AS IT EXISTS. AND I BELIEVE IN FOLLOWING CURRENT LAW.</u>

SO ALLOW ME TO REINFORCE: **GENERALLY, POLICE OFFICERS ARE NOT OUT ON THE STREETS TO GET PLEASURE OUT OF HURTING OR KILLING BLACK PEOPLE (OR ANY OTHER PEOPLE FOR THAT MATTER).** This is an **ABSOLUTE LIE.** And those who perpetrate this falsehood will certainly be dealt with very soon because it is putting our Black people in a hysterical state of mind; creating paranoia; and it is creating an unwarranted fear; which causes Blacks to do stupid things, and to react in wrongful ways when encountering Police, and thus get themselves injured or killed. **AND THIS SICK CYCLE IS RECURRING. THIS MUST STOP. THIS WILL STOP.**

SO NOW AGAIN, LISTEN TO THIS AND HEAR THIS CLEARLY: MANY OF OUR BLACK PEOPLE ARE GETTING THEMSELVES INJURED OR KILLED BECAUSE THEY HAVE BEEN FED LIES AND POISONOUS RHETORIC BY MISLED, CROOKED, DECEITFUL, AND/OR WEAK BLACK POLITICIANS, TREASONIST, RACE-BAITERS, RACE-HUSTLERS, BLACK-OPPORTUNIST, WHITE-OPPORTUNIST, LIARS, BLACK-RACIST, AND/OR OTHER SO-CALLED BLACK LEADERS. THESE BLACK PEOPLE LISTENING TO THESE LIES AND THIS POISONOUS RHETORIC HAVE BEEN MADE TO BELIEVE OR FEEL THAT THE POLICE ARE REALLY TRYING TO INJURE OR KILL THEM, AND THUS, WHEN THEY ARE STOPPED BY POLICE, BECAUSE OF THEIR ACTIONS AND REACTIONS UNDER THIS NEGATIVE PSYCHOLOGICAL STIMULI, IT DOES NOT GO WELL BECAUSE THEY DO NOT FULLY COOPERATE, OR DO THE THINGS MENTIONED ABOVE. AND ON THE REVERSE-SIDE, THIS SAME FOUL RHETORIC CAUSES TENSIONS AND MISTRUST ON BEHALF OF POLICE OFFICERS TOWARDS BLACK PEOPLE, AND IT PUTS POLICE OFFICERS ON HIGH-ALERT WHEN ENCOUNTERING BLACK PEOPLE, WHICH FURTHER INTENSIFIES AND EXACERBATES THE SITUATION CAUSING UNDUE INJURY, UNDUE VIOLENCE, AND/OR UNDUE DEATH ON BOTH SIDES. AND THEREFORE, THE TRUST-FACTOR BETWEEN BLACK PEOPLE AND THE POLICE IS VERY LOW, AND GETTING EVEN LOWER.

AND SADLY, THIS CREATES AN ONGOING AND RECURRING NEGATIVE DEBILITATING CYCLE OF MISTRUST, DISSENSION, AND DISCORD BETWEEN BLACK CITIZENS AND

POLICE OFFICERS IN WHICH BLACK PEOPLE END UP GETTING THEMSELVES INJURED OR KILLED. FURTHERMORE, SOMETIMES POLICE OFFICERS ARE GETTING INJURED OR KILLED IN THESE ENCOUNTERS AS WELL, OR IN OTHER SITUATIONS; AGAIN, BECAUSE OF THESE LIES AND FOUL RHETORIC.

AFTER READING OR BEING EXPOSED TO THIS BOOK, THE BLACK COMMUNITY WILL HAVE NO EXCUSES FOR NOT GIVING POLICE OFFICERS THEIR DUE HONOR AND RESPECT.

NEVERTHELESS, I CANNOT FEEL SORRY FOR CITIZENS, BLACK OR WHITE, WHO DO NOT FOLLOW THE LAWS OF A CIVILIZED SOCIETY, OR CITIZENS WHO ARE NOT AT LEAST WILLING TO FACE THEIR PUNISHMENT WHEN THEY ARE CAUGHT. But, most importantly, Black people need to stop feeding one-another lies and deceit, because ultimately Black people are getting the worse-end of these ordeals, most of the time. MOST POLICE OFFICER'S KNOW, OR HAVE BEEN TRAINED TO KNOW, OR SHOULD KNOW, THERE ARE MAJOR NEGATIVE REPERCUSSIONS FOR KILLING ANOTHER HUMAN-BEING; ESPECIALLY IF IT IS NOT JUSTIFIED. These negative repercussions are not only legal; they are also morally and psychologically disruptive to the killer as well.

IN OTHER WORDS, A PERSON'S LIFE IS NEVER THE SAME AGAIN AFTER THEY HAVE KILLED ANOTHER HUMAN BEING. THEIR LIFE IS USUALLY WAY MORE DISTURBED THAN BEFORE. SO, BE REST ASSURED THAT POLICE OFFICERS GENERALLY ARE NOT OUT TRYING TO SHOOT

AND KILL OTHER HUMAN-BEINGS, BLACK OR WHITE. AND BELIEVE ME, NO ONE CAN ESCAPE THE WRATH OF GOD FOR UNJUSTIFIED DELIBERATE MURDER; PLEASE DO NOT BE FOOLED.

AND ALSO, PLEASE REMEMBER, IT COULD BE SAID THAT THESE DEATHS COULD NOT HAPPEN IF GOD DID NOT ALLOW THEM. Yes, I believe there is a devil. However, the devil can only do what GOD allows him to do. Therefore, in my humble opinion, if GOD is allowing these injuries or killings to take place, it just might be our fault. And guess what, in many of these cases, it is true that Blacks are getting themselves injured or killed; then the mothers are crying; then the Black community is living with the misplaced sorrow, fear, and hysteria; and then some feed themselves and the Black community more lies. This is the very reason that some Black or low-income communities are run by criminals, and the community is living in fear and as somewhat hostages because Blacks continue to believe the lie that police are against them. They continue to feed the community the lie that the Police are the enemy, and therefore the Black community continues to suffer. It is very hard to empathize or sympathize with a person who refuses to do the right thing. A person like that is destined to continue to get him or herself in bad situations.

These lies that some Black people believe is another reason why a person like the Black Empire actor Jussie Smollett immediately gained sympathy from much of the Black community when he alluded that he was attacked by racist White Trump supporters. According to his television interview, Jussie Smollett claimed a racist attack against him by Whites involving an alleged noose or rope around his neck and stated that White men shouted that this is MAGA country. He also stated that they called him a faggot and a nigger, and that they poured bleach on him. However, authorities say Jussie Smollett filed a false police report. Jussie Smollett, after the fact, was indicted by a Cook County grand jury on 16 felony counts of disorderly conduct for allegedly lying about this incident.

However, as of about March 25, 2019, according to news sources, because Mr. Smollett agreed to do two days of community service and forfeited his $10,000 bond to pay court cost, the charges were dropped by the District Attorney's office. A Cook County First Assistant State's Attorney, Joseph Magats, stated during an interview that they do believe that Mr. Smollett did file a false police report and that the deal was not an exoneration of Mr. Smollett's actions. In other words, according to the District Attorney's Office, Mr. Smollett isn't considered innocent of the charges
(https://www.youtube.com/watch?v=x57fm8huEac&t=119s).

Therefore, based on the evidence that I have heard up to March 25, 2019, and based on Mr. Smollett's demeanor in his television interview up to that time, I personally believe he is guilty of filing a false police report for an alleged hate crime. Also, in my opinion, I believe some Blacks do some of the same types of things more often than one thinks to continually push the false narrative of White racism, and/or to take advantage of some aspect of the system. If it is ever determined by a criminal court or other legal entity that Jussie Smollett in-fact made a false police report for a hate crime, he should certainly be swiftly penalized in accordance to the law because these types of actions create discord, dissension, and it keeps hate alive in America. It also stifles race-relations by creating more distrust. These actions should be dealt with harshly and swiftly in accordance with current law.

In my opinion, another prime example of GOD'S wrath is in the city of Chicago (and some other American cities) where there is an astounding rate of young Black males killing one-another for no apparent reasons, and the Black Community in these areas are living in constant fear of death and/or injury. When one has no respect for structure or authority, this is what it boils down to. Some of these Black people had or have no respect for authority in their schools because the parents did not honor structure and authority. They had or have no respect for the Police or Government. They do not follow the rules or the law. So, now they are killing one-another on a daily-basis for no apparent reasons. These communities constantly live in sorrow and fear. The mothers are crying because their sons are being killed or injured by their own counterparts, and the mothers themselves live in constant fear and pain. What a shameful situation.

HOWEVER, I MUST REITERATE, HOW CAN WE HELP OR FEEL SORRY FOR PEOPLE WHO REFUSE TO HONOR BASIC HUMAN DECENCY, AND/OR REFUSE TO FOLLOW BASIC RULES AND LAWS; and further has accepted a lie that Police Officers are the enemy. It is difficult to do. And therefore, this ever-recurring cesspool of fear, destruction, and death is allowed to flourish and those very same Blacks who refuse to obey the law are reaping the whirlwind of this fear and death cesspool. Also, many District Attorneys, Detectives, Investigators, and Police Officers will tell you that it is very difficult to get Blacks from many of these communities to come forward with information about crimes or to get them to testify in court against a criminal. This further keeps crime alive and well in these communities.

> Proverbs chapter 28 verse 4 says "To complain about the law is to praise wickedness. To obey the law is to fight evil." And proverbs chapter 28 verse 9 says "GOD doesn't listen to the prayers of men who flout the law."

So, where can you get help if you cannot get it from the Police?

And believe me, one day you will need to call the Police. The low-income areas need Police probably more than any other communities because there is more crime there. Criminals do not want you to have any faith in the Police. In this way, they can take over the streets and the community.

SO THEREFORE, BASED ON WHAT HAS BEEN STATED ABOVE, MAYBE IT SHOULD OCCUR TO US THAT IF GOD IS ALLOWING US TO SUFFER, LIVE IN FEAR, AND BE KILLED AS A COMMUNITY; IT MIGHT BE SOMETHING THAT WE MAY BE DOING WRONG, OR ARE NOT DOING RIGHT. Shouldn't we think maybe there is something that we need to do differently so we can have no fear of death and sorrow like others living in peace?

Because remember, GOD is in control and continues to have all power at all times, from the beginning of time, and even today.

In the Bible, Romans chapter 13 verses 3-5 states:

> **"For the policeman does not frighten people who are doing right; but those doing evil will always fear him. So if you don't want to be afraid, keep the laws and you will get along well. The policeman is sent by GOD to help you. But if you are doing something wrong, of course you should be afraid, for he will have you punished. He is sent by GOD for that very purpose. Obey the laws, then, for two reasons: first, to keep from being punished, and second, just because you know you should."**

Therefore, in essence, it can be said, that generally, when one is fighting against the Police and law-and-order, they are fighting against GOD himself. Thus, there is no wonder some people are being injured or killed. No one can win fighting against the ALMIGHTY GOD. We should stop being fools and try to do the right thing and follow our laws that protect you and I. Or if you feel you must break the law to survive, at least sensibly accept the consequences when you are caught. Don't be a chump or a wimp about it. That is just common sense.

I know some people feel they must sale illegal drugs to survive and to make financial ends meet. I can empathize and understand their train of thought (although I do not condone it). However, do not become unduly violent towards a Police Officer if you are caught by police breaking the law. Deal with it in a sensible legal manner.

We have an incredible criminal justice system that strives to be fair. You will get a fair trial. And under President Trump, Congress has passed The First Step Act that is making the playing field more equal for Blacks and others who have possibly suffered some biases within the criminal justice system in the past.

AND LET ME LOUDLY AND CLEARLY SAY THIS: PLEASE STOP TEACHING OUR CHILDREN AND YOUNG ADULTS THAT THE POLICE OFFICER IS THEIR ENEMY—"BECAUSE HE OR SHE IS NOT."

When we do this we are certainly setting our children up for failure and creating unwarranted fear and paranoia; because generally, the Police Officer is never our enemy, unless we make him so. The Police Officer, in general, is to keep law-and-order, and thus, can be, and is our friend. So generally, the Police are our friends and our children's friends. So let us teach our children that the Police are their friends as long as they are following the law. And really, even when they are not following the law because they are there to correct them.

Furthermore, for you parents who let your children be in public with their buttocks or underwear being exposed (pants sagging); how do you think the police view this? The police do not view this in a positive manner I am sure.

Anyway, if a Black person, or any person for that matter, is doing what they are supposed to do and following the procedures and advice above, they have no reason to fear Police, to fear death, or to live in fear. Certainly, GOD will protect you. People do not realize that GOD and JESUS are always here and are still in control and they do not miss anything. GOD and JESUS have been here since the beginning of time and are still here on a consistent basis; constantly, currently, and eternally.

If you are following the law and have no ill intent and are doing what GOD would have you do, there is no need to fear the Police. And if you are following the law and acting responsibly when a police-encounter does occur, you have no reason to fear because you now know what to do. So do not put yourself in a bad situation with the Police. And remember, these laws apply to everyone, White and Black. I personally do not necessarily like police-encounters myself.

However, I personally do not fear the Police because I follow the law and I respect and obey them when those encounters do occur. Furthermore, I do not live in fear because I know when I am in a situation where criminals are trying to take over or harm me; I can and will call the Police and also defend myself in the process. The Police can be and are our protectors and friends. No person gets any joy or satisfaction out of taking another person's life; NO ONE.

NOW BASICALLY, THIS INFORMATION IS FOR THOSE WHO

WISH TO DO BETTER. THOSE WHO ARE CRIMINALS AND PREFER TO BE CRIMINALS AND ARE NOT TRYING TO DO THE RIGHT THING, IT IS INEVITABLE THAT YOU WILL PROBABLY CONTINUE TO DO SO, AND I AM NOT CONCERNED ABOUT YOU PER SE.

ALSO, SOMETIMES, WE AS CITIZENS SEE POLICE SHOOTINGS THAT LOOK VERY WRONG TO US ON THE SURFACE OR AT FIRST BLUSH. SUCH AS, WHEN SOMEONE IS SHOT IN THE BACK BY A POLICE OFFICER. WELL, IF WE DO NOT KNOW THE WHOLE STORY, AND/OR IF WE DID NOT SEE THE WHOLE TAPE, AND/OR IF WE DO NOT KNOW THE ENTIRE LAW; THIS COULD CERTAINLY LEAD US TO BELIEVE THAT THERE IS POLICE MISS-CONDUCT. IN A POLICE-ENCOUNTER, WHAT YOU THINK YOU SEE, MOST OF THE TIME IS NEVER THE WHOLE STORY.

Well, I have seen Police Officers shoot people in the back when they try to flee. It does look bad if you do not know the law and/or the whole situation. Nevertheless, there are times when a Police Officer may shoot a violent criminal in the back while the violent criminal is trying to flee. Those situations occur when a person is a violent danger to the general public; and/or that violent criminal is trying to escape from the police and that person is a violent danger to the general public, which means that if that violent criminal escapes out of the custody or eyesight of the Police Officer, he is likely to do serious bodily harm or kill someone else or take a hostage, which in-turn means that at that point the Police Officer generally has the right to use deadly force to stop that violent criminal by any means necessary under those dire circumstances.

This keeps that violent criminal from harming a hostage, or being able to do serious bodily harm to someone, or from killing someone. Or another example is if a criminal has been shooting at a Police Officer or at the public and he starts to run, at that point an Officer may shoot the violent criminal in the back to stop him from escaping, or to stop him from harming someone else, or from harming an Officer. These are situations in which a Police Officer is probably justified under the circumstances of shooting someone in the back. Therefore, under these types of situations and circumstances, it is very highly-likely that the violent suspect will injure or kill someone, because the violent suspect has already shown and proven that he will do bodily harm or kill someone. And thus, Police are more-than-likely allowed to shoot the violent suspect in the back to keep him from escaping and being able to violently harm or violently kill others.

And I will also say this: If you are sensitive and cannot accept some of the realities that situations like this present. Stay out of police business. Or to put it more bluntly: If you can't handle it, stay out of the way. Many times it is not pretty, however it is very very necessary.

IT LOOKS HORRIBLE WHEN YOU SEE A SITUATION LIKE THAT IF YOU DO NOT HAVE THE WHOLE STORY OR KNOW THE LAW. THAT'S WHY I SAY OVER AND OVER AGAIN: IF YOU DO NOT HAVE THE WHOLE STORY OR ALL THE FACTS ABOUT A SITUATION OR A POLICE-ENCOUNTER, OR IF YOU DO NOT UNDERSTAND THE LAW THOROUGHLY IN THE MATTER, IT IS BEST TO KEEP YOUR MOUTH CLOSED BECAUSE YOU ARE PROBABLY ONLY MAKING THINGS WORSE.

Furthermore, and most damningly, the false rhetoric and consistent lies revolving in the Black community is what is keeping the criminal element alive, keeping some Black communities living in fear of the Black criminals, and basically holding many Black communities hostage.

SO NOW, I SAY: YOU HAVE BEEN EDUCATED ON THE LAW FOR POLICE-ENCOUNTERS. I HAVE EXPLAINED THE LAW GENERALLY FOR POLICE-ENCOUNTERS AS BEST AS I KNOW IT. AT THIS TIME, I CHALLENGE YOU TO RE-EVALUATE SOME OF THE POLICE-ENCOUNTERS THAT YOU ARE AWARE OF FROM THE PAST AND MAKE A DECISION OF WHO WAS AT FAULT.

You may see things much differently or draw different conclusions now, or at least you certainly should, if you are honest with yourself. Some of these procedures or laws may seem unfair or skewed in favor of the Police.

However, the law is the law, and we must all respect and follow the law. Or if you think the law is unfair, take the proper channels to petition your legislature, or do what is necessary and try to have the law changed to reflect your view. That is the proper thing to do. Do not try to fight it within a police-encounter because the Police Officer is normally just doing his job. And remember, we the people have created these laws through the democratic and legislative process. THESE ARE THE LAWS AND RULES THAT WE HAVE VOTED FOR THROUGH OUR ELECTED REPRESENTATIVES -- THE MAJORITY RULES - AND THE DEMOCRACY RULES.

FINAL THOUGHTS ON POLICE-ENCOUNTERS:

LAW ENFORCEMENT AND GOVERNMENT OFFICIALS ARE THE MOST IMPORTANT ASPECTS AND COMPONENTS OF A CIVILIZED SOCIETY SUCH AS THE UNITED STATES OF AMERICA. It seems as though some Black and White people and others make every excuse they can to not follow the law and to not do the right thing. Let me make it clear, I have no sympathy or empathy for those who do not wish to follow and obey laws that promote peace and harmony among people in America. Those of you who think they do not have to respect or obey the rules or the law; you certainly do not have my support. Everyone must do their part.

WE CAN NEVER CLAIM "POLICE BRUTALITY" IF WE ARE NOT DOING OUR PART AND COOPERATING AS A CITIZEN SHOULD DO DURING THE POLICE-ENCOUNTER. SO AGAIN, JUST RELAX AND COOPERATE.

Also, I know there are times when Police may act inappropriately. In those cases, the Police Officer's should certainly be held accountable and punished accordingly.

HOWEVER, I STRONGLY FEEL THE POLICE OFFICER SHOULD BE GIVEN THE BENEFIT-OF-THE-DOUBT BECAUSE WE CERTAINLY NEED OUR POLICE. I WOULD RATHER HAVE THE POLICE IN MY SOCIETY THAN A CRIMINAL. ESPECIALLY IF THAT CRIMINAL WISHES TO MURDER AND DO PEOPLE SERIOUS PHYSICAL BODILY HARM.

I BELIEVE IN THE POLICE. I THINK THE MAJORITY OF POLICE OFFICERS ARE DECENT LAW-ABIDING CITIZENS. AND LASTLY, I WOULD RATHER HAVE A SOCIETY WITH POLICE OFFICERS, THAN WITHOUT. I would rather have a society where there may be a few bad Police Officers; rather than not having any Police Officers at all. This is not a perfect world and we cannot necessarily account for all those Police Officers who over-step their bounds. We can only punish them when we know this has occurred and it is proven within the ramifications of the law and police policy. But again, I believe this is in the minority.

Lastly, I certainly want to add, I know some people feel that the only way they can survive is by participating in activities that are against the law; such as selling drugs. Well, if that is what you feel you have to do to survive, that is your decision. It is a free society. However, why get mad, or be ugly, or nasty, or disrespectful, or uncooperative, or become violent, if you are caught by Police? The Police Officer is only doing his job. Furthermore, you will have your day in court. There is no need to be nasty or disrespectful. Please man-up or woman-up and accept the consequences of your actions and your behavior! We have a great criminal justice system. Take advantage of it.

Our system is predicated on fairness and due-process, unlike many other Countries. I know our system is not perfect. But, it is, by far, a heck-of-lot better than most, if not all Countries. Furthermore, I believe that our public school systems should have a course in police-encounters and/or a copy of this book incorporated into some of their courses.

And I know some say we need criminal justice reform because the criminal justice system is skewed against Blacks. And that very well may be true within some laws. However, that is another subject. This chapter only focuses on the police-encounter itself. And if you feel that way, start to petition your legislature and get involved to see that changes are made. If you are not trying to do something about it through the proper channels, please do not complain. We do not have a right to complain if we are not willing to do something ourselves to make things better, or are not willing to support someone who is trying to make things better.

Furthermore, the White House Administration under President Trump and Congress did actually work on Criminal Justice Reform and has made progress in this area. Again, under President Trump, Congress did recently pass The First Step Act that was aimed at making the playing field more equal for Blacks and others who have possibly suffered some biases within the criminal justice system in the past.

I have also had some Blacks tell me that I am siding with the Police or White people. Or that I am sounding as though I am against Black people. Please! Spare me of the nonsense! I side with the law and what is right in a civilized society. That's it. Keep the nonsense to yourself! It has nothing to do with Black or White, or siding with the Police.

It should be obvious why some White people do not want to live among certain other White and Black People who do not want to respect and/or obey the law and who choose to live life like heathens or animals. It should be obvious why some Black People do not want to live among certain other Black and White People who do not want to respect and/or obey the law and who choose to live life like heathens or animals. **EVERYONE IN AMERICA, HAS A SPIRITUAL AND LEGAL RIGHT TO LIVE AS THEY PLEASE.**

THEREFORE, IT SHOULD BE OBVIOUS WHY THOSE BLACK AND WHITE PEOPLE WHO CHOOSE TO LIVE IN PEACE AND HARMONY, AND WHO TRY TO AVOID CHAOS, DO NOT WISH TO LIVE AMONG THOSE WHO CHOOSE NOT TO ACCEPT THE TRUTH, OR RESPECT AND OBEY THE LAW. THESE PEOPLE WHO MOVE AWAY FROM THIS CHAOS ARE JUST EXERCISING COMMON SENSE AND THEIR RIGHTS.

Some Black and White people exercise their GOD-given rights and choose to live life in a more civilized manner and honor GOD and do good deeds and spread good-will. Why should they/we waste our time living among people who choose to live closer to the seedy side of life? WHY SHOULD WE/THEY WASTE OUR TIME AMONG PEOPLE WHO CHOOSE TO SPREAD HATE, LIES, DISSENSION, CHAOS, AND DISCORD? I CERTAINLY WILL NOT BE; ESPECIALLY WHEN THOSE PEOPLE REFUSE TO CHANGE.

IT SOMETIMES SEEM THAT ONCE A BLACK PERSON CHOOSES TO DO WHAT HE OR SHE FEELS IS THE RIGHT THING TO DO, AND LIVE IN A MANNER CONTRARY TO THE ABOVE CHAOS OR SPEAKS OUT AGAINST IT, SOME BLACKS CONSIDER HIM OR HER TO BE A UNCLE-TOM, A SELL-OUT TO THE BLACK RACE, A COON, AND/OR A LACKEY FOR WHITE PEOPLE, AND/OR OTHER DISRESPECTFUL TERMS.

But, who cares, if that person knows and feels they are doing the right thing? I certainly do not. It carries no weight with me.

> John chapter 8 verse 32 says ..."THE TRUTH WILL SET YOU FREE." And John chapter 8 verse 44 in essence says ...DON'T BE A "HATER OF TRUTH." AND Colossians chapter 3 verse 9 says "Don't tell lies to each other;"

NOW, you have been educated on what the law generally entails with police-encounters. You have been educated on what you generally can and cannot do. Therefore, it is up to you to do it.

> James Chapter 4 verse 17 says, "Remember, too, that knowing what is right to do and then not doing it is sin."

AT THE BEGINNING OF CHAPTER 4 THERE IS A VERY SHORT STORY ABOUT THE TEN GREEN MEN, & QUESTIONS AND ANSWERS THAT FOLLOW TO TEST YOUR LEARNING AND KNOWLEDGE ABOUT THIS TOPIC. PLEASE READ IT.

BOTTOM LINE: LEADERS ARE SUPPOSE TO BE FEARLESS, NOT FEARFUL. THERE ARE GOOD LEADERS AND BAD LEADERS. SOMETIMES IT IS DIFFICULT TO TELL WHICH IS WHICH. SOMETIMES TIMING IS ALSO A MAJOR FACTOR TO MAKE THESE DISTINCTIONS. NEVERTHELESS, BLACK LEADERS AND BLACK POLITICIANS NEED TO TELL BLACK PEOPLE THE TRUTH AND STOP FEEDING BLACK PEOPLE LIES, DECEIT, MISUNDERSTANDINGS, FALSE RHETORIC, AND GIVING THEM A PACIFIER AND A PASS. BLACK SO-CALLED LEADERS YOU SEEM TO FEAR YOUR OWN BLACK PEOPLE. BLACK LEADERS, YOU SEEM TO FEAR SOME TYPE OF BACKLASH FROM YOUR OWN BLACK COMMUNITY WHEN YOU TELL THEM THE TRUTH.

BLACK LEADERS STOP BEING COWARDS IN REGARDS TO SAYING AND DOING THE RIGHT AND PROPER THINGS AMONG FELLOW AMERICANS. OUT OF FEAR YOU LIE AND TELL A BLACK BOY HE IS A BLACK MAN. COWARDS, MALE OR FEMALE, ARE NOT WINNERS. COWARDS ARE LOSERS. COWARDS ARE FULL OF FEAR. FEAR IS NOT OF GOD. YOU CANNOT TRULY BE A TRUE LEADER IF YOU FEAR DOING THE RIGHT THING. WE ALL MUST RESPECT AND OBEY THE LAW AND TELL THE TRUTH. IF YOU CANNOT OR WILL NOT DO THIS, STEP-ASIDE AND LET SOMEONE ELSE WHO WILL FULFILL THAT ROLE.

IF YOU CANNOT CONDEMN RHETORIC OR BEHAVIOR FROM YOUR OWN BLACK COUNTER-PARTS THAT PROMOTES HATE AND DISCORD YOU ARE A POOR EXCUSE FOR A POLITICAL LEADER. YOU DO NOT NECESSARILY HAVE TO CONDEMN THE INDIVIDUAL, BUT YOU MUST CERTAINLY CONDEMN THE FOUL RHETORIC AND/OR THE FOUL BEHAVIOR IF YOU ARE A TRUE LEADER WHO WANTS TO SEE THIS NATION MOVE CLOSER TO GOD. HATE IS HATE, NO MATTER WHO IT COMES FROM. WE CANNOT PLAY FAVORITISM WITH HATE JUST BECAUSE THEY ARE BLACK LIKE US. LIFE AND LIVELIHOOD IS NOT A JOKE. IT IS VERY SERIOUS BECAUSE PRECIOUS LIVES ARE AT STAKE, AND GOD IS ALWAYS WATCHING; GOD NEVER SLEEPS NOR SLUMBERS. FOR "<u>HE</u>" IS "<u>THE CONSTANT!</u>"

CHAPTER 4: THE TEN GREEN MEN

At this point, I would like to take the time to tell everyone a "very short" fictional story about the 10 green men. At the end of this very short fictional story, I want to see if, Black people especially, will get the "message" of the story by answering the few questions at the end. However, anyone can participate.

THE STORY BEGINS AS FOLLOWS: In a certain American city there lived blue, purple, orange, and green men. There were 10 blue men, 10 purple men, 10 orange men, and 10 green men. All of the men of a certain color generally all looked the same. For example, all of the blue men basically looked alike, and so did all the other colored men within their particular color group. In this city, every time a crime was committed it was done by one of the green men. However, only seven of the ten green men would commit these crimes. The other three green men were not involved in committing any crimes. The crimes that were committed were violent crimes such as rape, armed robbery, assault, and murder.

Therefore, every time something negative happened or a crime was committed in this city, it was always committed by one of the seven green men. For example, a store owner was robbed at gunpoint by a green man on several occasions. One man was assaulted by one of these green men. A woman was raped by one of these green men. A man had been murdered by one of these green men. But, one of the most serious problems was that many Police Officers had been assaulted and some had been killed by some of these green men as well. The green men that were committing these crimes would always be combative, uncooperative, and would always physically fight against the Police when they were legally stopped or detained for any reason.

And again, many Police Officers had been assaulted and some had even been killed by these seven green men. Therefore, the police were very aware of the crimes and actions against Police by these seven green men and were very aware that these green men would cause problems during police-encounters as well.

Thus, whenever Police would encounter, detain, or investigate any of the green men they would use extra precautions and take extra measures to protect themselves because of past violence exerted against them by green men. For instance, when Police Officers encountered a green man they would be more on high-alert; they would be more cautious; they would try to take control of the situation quickly and more aggressively for their own safety; they would watch the green men closely; they would keep one hand on their weapon if necessary; sometimes they would secure them with hand-cuffs for the Officers safety; they would make sure that they could see the green man's hands; amongst other things to ensure that the Police Officer was safe.

But remember, three of the ten green men were not a part of the criminal acts. Nevertheless, when the other three green men were stopped by the Police, they too were treated in the same manner because they were green. These three green men did not approve of the criminal acts that the other seven green men were committing. However, remember, all the green men generally looked the same and the Police could not tell them apart.

So whenever the Police encountered a green man they were always on high alert; and would take extra precautions and extra measures as stated above whether it was one of the seven bad green men actually committing the crimes, or the three good green who were not, because again, they could not tell them apart.

The three green men complained about this and felt they were being discriminated against or treated wrongfully because they had committed no crimes.

UNDER THE CIRCUMSTANCES ABOVE ABOUT THE TEN GREEN MEN, PLEASE ANSWER THE FOLLOWING QUESTIONS:

There are not necessarily any exact right or wrong answers to these questions. However, there are some proposed correct answers that are given after the questions and are considered to be the best answers. These questions are to make you think based on the literature you have just read in this book, but specifically, think about the literature you read in this book about police-encounters and The Ten Green Men.

1. Are the Police Officers wrong or in error for taking extra precautions when encountering all green men?

2. Do the three good green men have a legitimate complaint about the extra precautions that the Police are taking when they encounter all green men?

3. Are the three good green men being discriminated against or being treated unfairly by the Police?

4. Would it be a good idea for the three good green men to try to persuade the other seven bad green men to obey the law or to speak out against them?

5. Should the three good green men disapprove of the Police for the treatment and the extra precautions taken by the Police when they encounter all green men under these circumstances?

6. Should the three good green men disapprove the behavior and take some type of actions against the seven bad green men under these circumstances?

THE BEST ANSWERS ARE AS FOLLOWS:

1. No. The Police Officers are not wrong or in error for taking extra precautions when encountering all green men because Police Officers should and also do have the right to take extra precautions to protect themselves if they feel there is a present threat, or a potential present threat. Police have every right to protect themselves as they exercise their sworn duties to enforce the law.

2. No. The three good green men do not have a legitimate complaint about the extra precautions that the Police are taking when they encounter all green men. Although the three green men's complaints can be understood, nevertheless they should put themselves in the Officer's shoes. Empathy goes a long way in this situation. The three good green men must understand that the Police Officers do not know them from the other seven bad green men, and the Officers are only trying to protect themselves and the public while doing their job. The three good green men just happen to be a part of a group of people who are choosing not to obey the law, which makes things more uncomfortable for them because they are a part of this same group.

3. No. The three good green men are not being discriminated against or being treated unfairly by the Police because, again, the three good green men just happen to be a part of a group of people who are making it more difficult for them. The Police cannot distinguish the three good green men from the seven bad green men. Therefore, the Police must take these extra precautions against all green men.

4. Yes. It would be a good idea for the 3 good green men to try to persuade the other seven bad green men to obey the law or to speak out against them because we must all fight

against the evils or negative behaviors among our own groups, tribes, and races. Every race of people, or political group, or organization must fight the evil and unethical behaviors amongst itself. This is the only way that our world and communities get better; and not worse. Again, if they can, they should persuade, convince, or fight against the other seven bad green men in some legal manner so the other seven bad green men will start to obey the law. In this way, it makes the whole group of green men better men and the whole situation better.

5. No. The three good green men should not disapprove of the Police for the treatment and the extra precautions taken by the Police when they encounter all green men under these circumstances because the Police are just doing their job while trying to protect themselves and the public. There is only so much that the Police can do as they exercise their duties. Police have the right to protect themselves by any means necessary as they exercise their sworn duties to enforce the law. This is not a perfect world and we must sometimes recognize that others can, and most of the times do, make things more difficult for us if we are a part of that particular group.

6. Yes. The three good green men should disapprove the behavior and take some type of actions against the seven bad green men under these circumstances because the seven bad green men are making life more difficult for the three good green men. That is why it is important to support truth, facts, and justice; and to fight against evil and injustices at all times because eventually, it affects us all.

Dr. Martin Luther King Jr. once said "Injustice anywhere is a threat to justice everywhere. We are caught in an inescapable network of mutuality, tied in a single garment of destiny. Whatever affects one directly, affects all indirectly." …"This is the way God's universe is made; this is the way it is structured."

The message of this section about The Ten Green Men is to create a better understanding for people who come from a specific race, such as Black people, to see that if you are a part of a group of people and the majority of them are not willing to follow procedures during police-encounters; if you are a part of that group then generally it can and possibly will have some type of effect on you. It will possibly have an effect on you just because you are identified as part of that group. That is basically just a fact of life and reality. Thus, we must take action within our own groups to make the group better. We cannot stand by and condone behavior that we know is morally, ethically, or legally wrong.

This also can and does apply in civil matters, business matters, social matters, politics, Hollywood, and other aspects of life. We must all do our part.

ALSO, WE AS BLACK PEOPLE NEED TO STOP SO EASILY AND FALSELY CLAIMING RACISM, CALLING PEOPLE RACIST, CLAIMING WHITE SUPREMACY, AND CLAIMING A RACIST SYSTEM WHEN IT DOES NOT APPLY TO THE CIRCUMSTANCES OR SITUATION, AND/OR WHEN WE HAVE NO CONCRETE AND UNDENIABLE PROOF. IT CAN BE SUCH AN INSULT TO SOMEONE INNOCENT; IT IS VERY WRONG, AND FURTHER A SIN AND NOT OF GOD.

A BRIEF SYNOPSIS ABOUT A WEALTHY BLACK AMERICAN WOMAN:

I read a story in a news account about a very wealthy Black American celebrity Female. I do not wish to call her name for various reasons. Furthermore, she is someone I greatly admire and respect. She is probably one of the wealthiest and most influential Black celebrity women living in America. Nevertheless, according to the story she was in a foreign country and she went into an upscale store to look around and/or to shop. She saw a very attractive item that she asked the seller to take down from a wall so she could more closely examine and feel it.

The seller told her no it was too expensive. According to the story, the Black celebrity asked a second time to examine the item and the seller continued to say no, telling the celebrity that the item she wanted to see was too expensive and that she would not be able to afford it. The seller further explained why the item was so expensive. Also, the seller herself was embarrassed by the expensive price of the item. It is quite obvious, according to the news account, that the seller was just a salesperson and did not set the prices.

Thus, the Seller then showed the Black celebrity other similar items that were not as expensive. But, according to the story, the Black celebrity asked a third time, and the seller said she did not want to hurt the Black celebrity's feelings. The Seller acted this way only because the seller felt the Black celebrity woman would see the price and be disappointed and her feelings would be hurt as past customers had been because the item was too expensive and she would not be able to afford it.

So, for these reasons, the seller decided not to take the item down for this particular Black celebrity woman because she felt the same thing was going to happen again. The seller did not want to see another disappointed face. Therefore, again, to avoid this from happening, the seller tried to convince the Black woman that the item she wanted to see was not worth the Black woman's time. So the seller tried to show her other items of similarity.

Let me remind you that the seller did not know that this Black woman was a wealthy and famous Celebrity in America and that she could actually afford the item. She only knew that the item was extremely expensive and that other similar items were cheaper and she did not want to experience another disappointed and sad face.

Well, the sad and disappointing part of the story is this: the wealthy Black Celebrity women contributed this situation to racism. The seller also even explained after the fact, that the seller herself felt that the item was too expensive and other similar items were not. Thus, this situation had nothing to do with prejudice, racism, hate, or extreme bias. And again, it is obvious, that this seller was just a sales person, and she herself felt the item was too expensive, and she herself did not set the prices.

Based on the fact that I have great respect for this Black celebrity woman and have seen her advance the cause of humanity, it is very sad and bewildering to me that this Black Celebrity concluded that this situation was about racism. Maybe the celebrity was just having a bad day. But, in my opinion, it was clearly not about racism. And I find it very difficult to see how the celebrity could have concluded such a determination based on the facts.

Furthermore, if the Celebrity wanted to stop all the confusion and avoid such a negative conclusion and news account, the first time the seller told her that the item was too expensive; the celebrity could have easily assured her that she could afford it by exposing her credentials or by other means.

On the second request, when the seller told her the item cost too much, again the Celebrity could have assured her that she could afford it. On the third request, when the seller told her that she didn't want to hurt her feelings, the celebrity could have assured the seller that she would not hurt the celebrity's feelings, and again assured the seller that she was capable of affording the item. This could have resolved all issues. But instead, on the third response from the seller, the Black Celebrity actually said to the Seller "you are probably right, I can't afford it" and walked out of the store.

In my opinion, the Black Celebrity could have really made an effort to dilute the situation; especially if she was going to make this a negative public story about racism that I feel could have been avoided, and that actually had no merit. Thus, this issue could have easily been resolved even if she did not buy the item. In my opinion, the Black celebrity was in gross error to claim that this was a racist issue. There were many other rational explanations that could have been concluded in this situation other than the negative determination that it was about racism, that it was racially motivated, or about race prejudice.

We, as Blacks, need to stop immediately drawing such negative conclusions about such simple situations and matters. Situations that we ourselves could resolve without making others feel bad who had pure and sincere intentions. According to the facts of this story, the seller seemed to have no ill intent. And again, I am really very shocked that this particular Black celebrity drew the conclusion that this was a racist moment or situation.

The point goes back to **THE TEN GREEN MEN.** It is not always about the negative stigmas of prejudice and racism. But anyway, this very powerful influential Black woman comes back to America and tells the story as though it was about racism. This in-turn influences other Blacks to feel that racism is more prevalent in the world than it really is, and it hurts us as a people, and it hurts race-relations in America and in the world. For this very influential Black woman to draw that conclusion is allowing Satan to cause us to draw the worst conclusions possible. Then that Black woman's power and influence rubs off on poor, middle-class, and other Blacks and they feel that racism is still very alive and well to a degree that it is not. What a horrible decision to make under such a simple situation. It is very disappointing to me because this situation could have been easily handled much better.

As I have stated in the chapter called **UNINFORMED AND IGNORANT CELEBRITIES:** Celebrities have a much greater responsibility for what they say, and for the decisions that they make because it influences other people in masses. GOD will hold them more responsible.

Therefore, for this Black female Celebrity to make this out to be a race issue and to attribute it to prejudice, racism, hate, or extreme bias is so very unfortunate, very disturbing, and very disappointing. **THESE TYPES OF UNWARRANTED STATEMENTS ADD TO SATAN'S REPERTOIRE AND EVIL BAG OF TRICKS TO KEEP US DIVIDED AND DISTRUSTFUL OF ONE-ANOTHER, AND TO FURTHER KEEP THE HORRIBLE LIE OF RACISM AND THE HATE IT BELLOWS ALIVE. PLEASE, LET'S CLEAN IT UP BLACK PEOPLE.**

THE MYTH THAT BLACKS MUST DO A BETTER JOB THAN WHITES:

I am sure most people and Blacks have heard the saying that a Black and White can have the same position, responsibilities, or a certain task; however, the Black person has to do it better than the White person. The message in **THE TEN GREEN MEN** also addresses this issue. Many Blacks say that when a Black person has a position, responsibilities, or a certain task, they have to do it much better than a White. Well, if seven Blacks in the same position before you really did a bad job, or were deceitful, or were hateful and untrustworthy; common sense should tell you that if you are Black you should expect to be scrutinized more based upon what the other seven Blacks did who came before you. It is really just common sense that if I have experienced 7 green men who are foul people, whenever I see a green man I am going to be on the defense or more careful. This is just human nature. This is just common human behavior. This is just common sense. It has nothing to do with racism, prejudice, and/or hate.

Same with Blacks. This really should not bother you. This should not make you angry. If you are Black, you should be willing to prove yourself under these circumstances. This would be no big deal for someone with proper intentions. It certainly does not bother me. It certainly would not make me angry at the employer, because really, the other seven Blacks have made it harder on me, not the one that is employing me or trusting me to do the task. The other seven Blacks have created an impression that Blacks are this way and have made it more difficult for me. So, in order for me to prove different, I must <u>do</u> differently. I will show them what <u>I</u> can do and show them that some of us Blacks will do it right. We should stop pouting and acting as though we do not have some foul acting Black people within our race.

We as Blacks ALL know that there are some good-for-nothing untrustworthy Blacks running rampant in the Black community and in some of our black families; Blacks who do things sloppily at best; Blacks who are lazy; and/or Blacks who do not honor or follow the rules or the law if they can avoid it. Just as Whites ALL know that there are some good-for-nothing untrustworthy Whites running rampant in the White community and within some of their white families; Whites who do things sloppily at best; Whites who are lazy; and/or Whites who do not honor or follow the rules or the law if they can avoid it.

The basic difference between the Whites and the Blacks is this: we as Blacks seem to have more Blacks being mischievous and doing more wrong within our race than Whites do within their race. In other words, the masses of Blacks, or the overwhelming majority of Blacks seem to be engaged in foolishness and not following GOD, or not following the rules and the laws, or not exhibiting basic human decency; moreso than the overwhelming majority of Whites. This is why the overwhelming majority of Blacks are not finding favor with GOD and are not financially stable because they have the wrong mindset. On the reverse side, this is why the overwhelming majority of Whites are finding favor with GOD and are financially stable. GOD is judging us and granting rewards or punishment accordingly and currently TODAY. HE is not only anticipating JUDGMENT DAY, but he is also giving us partially what is due to us right now, and in a very certain sense, it is JUDGMENT DAY. Whites seem to be doing better than us as a race, in a certain sense, because of these facts.

All I am saying here is, we as Blacks, need to start being more civil within America, so we can reap more benefits from America, and from GOD. So again, as Blacks, we need to fight against the negative behaviors within our own race.

[113]

We need to clean ourselves up. We need to rid our race of as much evil as possible. We need to refute and rebuke bad behavior. We need to shun and shame foul and unwarranted behavior. We need to stop the blame-game and take responsibility for our own actions and for our own communities. We need to embarrass foul behavior and look down upon it. We need to cause Black people to be ashamed of being foul and disgraceful. WE NEED TO REBUKE SATAN AND EMBRACE THE WILL OF GOD. AND GUESS WHAT, IT IS CERTAINLY ABOUT TO HAPPEN.

BOTTOM LINE:

POLICE OFFICERS; WE THANK YOU FOR YOUR SERVICE. PLEASE CONTINUE TO DO YOUR JOB AND ENFORCE THE LAW AS YOU HAVE SWORN TO DO. WE'VE GOT YOUR BACK! WE WILL NEVER ALLOW HOODLUMS AND THUGS TO OVERRUN THE AMERICAN SOCIETY AND THE AMERICAN WAY OF LIFE; BLACK OR WHITE!

BLACK PEOPLE (ALL PEOPLE): WE SHOULD NEVER FEAR TO REACH OUT TO GET HELP FROM OTHERS. WHETHER THAT HELP IS SPIRITUAL, PSYCHOLOGICAL, MENTAL, EMOTIONAL, PHYSICAL, OR EVEN FINANCIAL. WE ALL NEED HELP SOMETIMES. AT THOSE TIMES, WE MUST BE HUMBLE AND SMART ENOUGH TO REACH OUT TO GET THE NECESSARY HELP WE THINK WE MAY NEED. DO NOT BE AFRAID TO REACH OUT AND ASK FOR HELP OR TO GET THERAPY OR TO CONFIDE OR TALK WITH SOMEONE YOU CAN TRUST. IT COULD VERY WELL SAVE YOUR/OUR LIFE.

CONCLUSION AND FINAL MESSAGES

I TRY TO END ALL OF MY BOOKS WITH A POSITIVE, INSPIRING, AND MOTIVATIONAL MESSAGE. IN THIS BOOK, I PLAN TO DO THE SAME. BUT, AT THE SAME TIME, I MUST REITERATE THE CORE MESSAGES OF THIS BOOK TO MANY BLACK PEOPLE, BECAUSE THE MESSAGES ARE VERY IMPORTANT.

FINAL MESSAGE TO BLACK LEADERS AND BLACK POLITICIANS

BOTTOM LINE: LEADERS ARE SUPPOSE TO BE FEARLESS, NOT FEARFUL. THERE ARE GOOD LEADERS AND BAD LEADERS. SOMETIMES IT IS DIFFICULT TO TELL WHICH IS WHICH. SOMETIMES TIMING IS ALSO A MAJOR FACTOR TO MAKE THESE DISTINCTIONS. NEVERTHELESS, BLACK LEADERS AND BLACK POLITICIANS NEED TO TELL BLACK PEOPLE THE TRUTH AND STOP FEEDING BLACK PEOPLE LIES, DECEIT, MISUNDERSTANDINGS, FALSE RHETORIC, AND GIVING THEM A PACIFIER AND A PASS. BLACK SO-CALLED LEADERS YOU SEEM TO FEAR YOUR OWN BLACK PEOPLE. BLACK LEADERS, YOU SEEM TO FEAR SOME TYPE OF BACKLASH FROM YOUR OWN BLACK COMMUNITY WHEN YOU TELL THEM THE TRUTH.

BLACK LEADERS STOP BEING COWARDS IN REGARDS TO SAYING AND DOING THE RIGHT AND PROPER THINGS AMONG FELLOW AMERICANS. OUT OF FEAR YOU LIE AND TELL A BLACK BOY HE IS A BLACK MAN. COWARDS, MALE OR FEMALE, ARE NOT WINNERS. COWARDS ARE LOSERS. COWARDS ARE FULL OF FEAR. FEAR IS NOT OF GOD. YOU CANNOT TRULY BE A TRUE LEADER IF YOU FEAR DOING THE RIGHT THING. WE ALL MUST RESPECT AND OBEY THE LAW AND TELL THE TRUTH. IF YOU CANNOT OR WILL NOT DO THIS, STEP-ASIDE AND LET SOMEONE ELSE WHO WILL FULFILL THAT ROLE.

IF YOU CANNOT CONDEMN RHETORIC OR BEHAVIOR FROM YOUR OWN BLACK COUNTER-PARTS THAT PROMOTES HATE AND DISCORD YOU ARE A POOR EXCUSE FOR A POLITICAL LEADER. YOU DO NOT NECESSARILY HAVE TO CONDEMN THE INDIVIDUAL, BUT YOU MUST CERTAINLY CONDEMN THE FOUL RHETORIC AND/OR THE FOUL BEHAVIOR IF YOU ARE A TRUE LEADER WHO WANTS TO SEE THIS NATION MOVE CLOSER TO GOD. HATE IS HATE, NO MATTER WHO IT COMES FROM. WE CANNOT PLAY FAVORITISM WITH HATE JUST BECAUSE THEY ARE BLACK LIKE US. LIFE AND LIVELIHOOD IS NOT A JOKE. IT IS VERY SERIOUS BECAUSE PRECIOUS LIVES ARE AT STAKE, AND GOD IS ALWAYS WATCHING; GOD NEVER SLEEPS NOR SLUMBERS. FOR HE IS THE CONSTANT!

MY FINAL MESSAGE TO BLACK PEOPLE

TOO MANY OF US BLACK PEOPLE HAVE LIFE AND REALITY MISCONSTRUED OR MISINTERPRETED. THIS MESSAGE IS "ONLY" TO THOSE WHOM IT APPLIES.

Stop being liars. Stop hating. Get rid of the hate-blinders and the evil skim or scales over your eyes so you can see clearly and visualize what America has to offer, and thus be blessed. Stop living and focusing on things of the past that create or exacerbate hate. That is a sin. There is no place in anyone's personal life or profession to exhibit HATE towards any other human-being; NEVER. Hate is always the wrong answer no matter how colorful we make it. Hate is never the way no matter how we try to justify it, Black or White. When it comes to the word HATE, it should never be used or expressed towards anyone in the human-race; PERIOD. It has no place in that sphere. It should not be a part of our vocabulary at all when speaking about any other human-being.

This word hate alone will certainly lead you down the wrong path here on this earth, in the hereafter, and straight to hell. And remember, that is where Satan wants us, in hell with him, or when he goes back. So, it is not by accident that he puts that word in our mouths so quickly.

ALSO, THERE IS NO WONDER WHY <u>SATAN</u> WANTS
TO KEEP US ANGRY, BITTER, AND MAD AT WHITE
PEOPLE AND/OR THE US GOVERNMENT BECAUSE
IN THAT WAY HE HAS MORE CONTROL OVER US SO
HE CAN CONTINUE TO LEAD US TOWARDS
ETERNAL DAMNATION. SATAN IS THE ARCHITECT
AND ENGINEER IN WHAT HE DOES. HE IS THE BEST
IN DOING EVIL AND GETTING OTHERS TO DO EVIL.

Start obeying and/or at the least respecting Police Officers, the government and its Officials, and authority. There is nothing wrong with being courteous to Police Officers and Government Officials. Actually, it is our duty as being a part of the human-race to do so. That is why we have a system. Our system is structured and founded upon rules and laws that basically stem directly from biblical principles.

> **As Paul wrote to Titus in Titus Chapter 3 verse 1, "Remind your people to obey the government and its officers,…" Furthermore, Romans chapter 13 verse 7 says "…obey those over you, and give honor and respect to all those whom it is due."**

We are to obey the government and its elected officers. If we do not like them, next time, vote them out of office, if possible. If you think the law is wrong or unfair, work through the proper channels to have the law changed. We have an inclusive system; use it!

AND STOP FALSELY CLAIMING RACISM, STOP EASILY AND FALSELY CALLING WHITE PEOPLE AND OTHERS RACIST, STOP CLAIMING WHITE SUPREMACY, A RACIST SYSTEM, AND RESENTING WHITE PEOPLE AND THE US GOVERNMENT FOR SHALLOW-MINDED AND UN-WARRANTED REASONS OR WITHOUT ABSOLUTE CONCRETE JUSTIFICATIONS. STOP WRONGFULLY PREJUDGING OR PASSING JUDGMENT ON WHITE PEOPLE; WE ARE NOT GOD.

STOP PLAYING THE RACE-CARD. LET US STOP DRAWING STEADFAST CONCLUSIONS ON POLICE-ENCOUNTERS OR COURT CASES WE DO NOT HAVE THE WHOLE STORY ABOUT OR ALL THE EVIDENCE AND FACTS ABOUT. LET THE SYSTEM, THROUGH OUR GRAND JURY'S AND JURY'S, HANDLE THESE AS OUR SYSTEM IS DESIGNED TO DO. LET'S STOP PLAYING THE BLAME-GAME. LET'S ANALYZE OURSELVES FIRST AND FOREMOST.

Let us stop making steadfast judgments on the law if we do not know the particular law thoroughly. Stick to your craft. Stay in your lane. Stop making or taking steadfast positions on political issues when you do not know or understand the full political issue or situation thoroughly. Stick to your profession. These behaviors have no sort of long-term rewards for us. These behaviors make us ugly and displeasing to others in a civilized society. Changing from these ill behaviors will bring us short-term, long-term, and eternal rewards. BELIEVE ME!!!

GET OFF THE FRONTLINES OF AMERICAN LIFE IF YOU ARE NOT WILLING TO BE FAIR AND JUST, OR WE WILL REPLACE YOU. GIVE CREDIT "WHERE" CREDIT IS DUE. GIVE CREDIT "WHEN" CREDIT IS DUE. REMEMBER, NO ONE IS ALL BAD ALL THE TIME, AND THERE IS USUALLY SOME GOOD IN EVERYONE. SUPPORT WHAT BENEFITS AMERICA AND THE HUMAN-RACE.

Live in the present. Recognize that we all have biases. Recognize that this is not nor will it ever be a perfect world for Blacks or Whites; NEVER. That is not what this life is necessarily about.

Recognize the blessings we really have by being in America. Recognize the opportunities we have in America and do not squander the talents and gifts that GOD has given you. Take advantage of opportunities when they come. Opportunities will not come all the time. Count your blessings and be thankful for whatever you have. There is always someone worse off than you are; ALWAYS!

IF WE WOULD RID OURSELVES OF SUCH NEGATIVE UNSUBSTANTIATED BAGGAGE, WE WOULD BE ABLE TO BETTER SEE THAT AMERICAN LIFE HAS SO MUCH GOOD TO

OFFER US. AND FURTHERMORE, GOD WILL GIVE US OUR
SPECIFIC DIRECTION FOR OUR OWN PERSONAL LIVES. BUT,
HE WILL NOT DO IT IF WE CONTINUE TO HATE AND WILL NOT
ACCEPT THE TRUTH. AND REMEMBER, AMERICA IS "OUR"
COUNTRY AS WELL TO MAKE IT BETTER, AND TO EXTRACT
BLESSINGS FROM IT AS APPLICABLE. THIS COUNTRY
BELONGS TO US BLACKS JUST AS IT DOES TO WHITES.

WE ARE ONE OF THE **"ORIGINAL"** AMERICANS. HOWEVER,
THAT MEANS NOTHING IF WE ARE GOING TO CONTINUE TO
BE UNPATRIOTIC, FOUL, AND IRRATIONAL. THERE ARE NO
BLESSINGS IN THAT. SO, ENGAGE AMERICA, LEARN IT,
AND BENEFIT FROM IT.

Calling someone a racist or claiming white supremacy without
proof is very easy. However, it is very lazy, irresponsible, wrong,
evil, and foul. Remember, we all must be personally judged by
GOD through his Son JESUS CHRIST some day; Black and
White, Jews and Gentiles, Master and Slave, Rich and Poor, Strong
and Weak, Lazy and Robust, Good and Evil. Remember, we are
all a part of the human family. If you are not dancing to GOD'S
tune, to some degree or another, no matter how minute it is, you
are certainly destined to fail; and you are definitely not playing the
winning-hand.

AND ONCE AGAIN, IT IS VERY IMPORTANT TO BE ABLE TO
EMPATHIZE WITH OTHERS. Always be able to empathize with
others, and for others. Always be able to put yourself in someone
else's shoes. Always be able to empathize with your opponent or
adversary. Sometimes it is a mistake to be too critical or too
steadfast. **As humans, we must remain somewhat flexible,
pliable, and open to allowing others an opportunity to correct**

themselves. **This is very important. To truly be a great person or great leader, one must have the ability to empathize with and for others.** If not, one can never be great, because, in essence, both persons or both sides could very well be right or reasonable even though their views or resolves are different. There is a very true statement that says "reasonable minds can differ." *Therefore, a little empathy can bridge the gap of disharmony, & bring about peace and/or synergy between the two opposing parties or people.*

Anyway, back to this, how would you feel if someone concludes or deems you a racist, or a liar, or a thief based upon what someone else has said; or based upon what the fake media has reported; or without proper proof? I am sure you would not like it. So, please show the same common courtesy and respect for others before condemning them. That especially applies to hearing stories in the news media because there is a whole lot of fake-news out there.

ALSO, AS LONG AS WE ARE ON THIS EARTH AND ARE IN THIS FIRST BODY, WE WILL ALWAYS HAVE OUR OWN PERSONAL DEMONS TO FIGHT. AND WE EACH PERSONALLY NEED HELP TO FIGHT SATAN. THAT IS WHY WE NEED TO HAVE GOD AS OUR BACK-UP. WITHOUT HIM, WE HAVE NO CHANCE; NONE! GOD IS THE ONLY ONE THAT CAN PROTECT US FROM SATAN'S GRIP.

Nevertheless, anyone with common sense is able to determine what the truth is, and what is not. And as the Bible says, generally, we all innately know the difference between right and wrong. And thus, we have no excuse to continue in abject and/or foul behavior.

> **Again, James Chapter 4 verse 17 says, "Remember, too, that knowing what is right to do and then not doing it is sin."**

SO, BLACK PEOPLE, PLEASE LET US NOT DECIDE TO BE A SCOURGE UPON THE EARTH. PLEASE DO NOT DECIDE TO BE A SCOURGE IN THE EYESIGHT OF THE ALMIGHTY GOD. OUR OPPORTUNITY TO BE A GREAT PEOPLE AND TO EFFECT POSITIVE CHANGE IN AMERICA IS UPON US. MANY OF US ARE BLOWING OUR OPPORTUNITY BY ENGAGING IN HATE AND FOOLISHNESS.

PLEASE DO NOT BLOW YOUR OPPORTUNITY TO MAKE AMERICA A BETTER PLACE TO LIVE. I REPEAT: Stop being cowards in regards to saying and doing the right and proper things among fellow Americans and in life. Cowards, male or female, are not winners. Cowards are losers. Cowards are full of fear. Fear is not of GOD. Don't you want to be proud and feel good about yourself? I know I do.

AND MOST IMPORTANTLY, LET US STOP SO EASILY AND FALSELY SCREAMING RACISM, CALLING PEOPLE RACIST, CLAIMING WHITE SUPREMACY, AND CLAIMING A RACIST SYSTEM WHEN IT DOES NOT APPLY TO THE CIRCUMSTANCES OR SITUATION, AND/OR WHEN WE HAVE NO CONCRETE AND UNDENIABLE PROOF. IT CAN BE SUCH AN INSULT TO SOMEONE INNOCENT; IT IS VERY WRONG, AND FURTHER A SIN AND NOT OF GOD.

This message is really only for those Blacks who want to do better and have a more quality life and live by righteous principles. For those who do not, I am not concerned about you. You will certainly get what you deserve, and I will definitely be one of those who will assist and push in that effort to ensure you do.

THEREFORE, BLACK PEOPLE, ULTIMATELY, LET US STOP ALLOWING SATAN TO USE US IN THESE HATEFUL MANNERS. LET US STOP ALLOWING OURSELVES TO BE USED TO NEGATIVELY BURDEN DOWN AMERICA. SATAN HAS BEEN USING SOME OF US FOR FAR TOO LONG. SATAN HAS BEEN PLAYING MANY OF US BLACKS FOR SUCKERS AT HIS WHIM. THERE ARE NO ETERNAL BENEFITS OR REWARDS FOR BEING A SERVANT, EMPLOYEE, OR INDEPENDENT-CONTRACTOR FOR SATAN.

LET US BE PART OF THE SOLUTION, RATHER THAN PART OF THE PROBLEM IN AMERICA. GOD IS NOT PLAYING WITH YOU! GOD IS NOT PLAYING WITH ME! GOD IS NOT PLAYING WITH US!

WE AS BLACKS "MUST" DO MUCH BETTER. WE AS BLACKS "CAN" DO MUCH BETTER. WE AS BLACKS "WILL" DO MUCH BETTER.

LET US NOT BE THE THISTLES AMONG THE WHEAT THAT JESUS SPOKE ABOUT IN MATTHEW CHAPTER 13 VERSES 37-42. LET US NOT BECOME CITIZENS OF HELL AS PROVERBS CHAPTER 9 VERSE 18 TALKS ABOUT. RATHER, LET US BE PART OF THE SALT, OR SEASONING, OR LIGHT OF THE WORLD THAT JESUS SPOKE ABOUT IN MATTHEW CHAPTER 5 VERSES 13 THROUGH 16. LET US STOP ALLOWING SATAN THE POWER TO RELEGATE US TO CONTINUE TO BE THE LAST IN LINE. HOW DO WE ACCOMPLISH THIS? BY OBEYING THE UNIVERSAL AND MORAL ORDER OF LIFE AND BY YIELDING TO GOD.

NO ONE HAS MORE POWER OVER YOU THAN YOU, OR SATAN, OR GOD! BUT, IF YOU HAVE GOD, HE WILL PROTECT YOU FROM ALLOWING SATAN TO TOTALLY OVER-POWER YOU. IF WE APPLY THE INFORMATION ABOVE, GREATER DAYS ARE AHEAD FOR US ALL, BLACK AND WHITE! START ENGAGING IN AMERICA FOR POSITIVE CHANGE BLACK AMERICAN; AS YOU KNOW YOU CAN! AND DO NOT LET ANYONE, BLACK OR WHITE, DIM OR DAMPEN YOUR GOD-GIVEN LIGHT AND SPIRIT!!!

THANK YOU

I would like to thank you once again for purchasing this book. It is my sincere hope that this book has exposed you to some truths and facts that will give you more inspiration and confidence for living a more quality life. I have used scriptures of the Bible, my Professional education, science, the law, police policies, public policies, and basic common sense and common knowledge to support all of the messages in this book. I have read the Bible's Old Testament in full from begging to end in sequence on at least four separate occasions. I have read the Bible's New Testament in full from begging to end in sequence on about seven separate occasions. I have a Bachelor's degree in Political Science (focus on the Presidency). I have my Juris Doctorate Degree in Juris Prudence (the study of law). I researched all of the bodies of information and law mentioned above to confirm and to support all of my contentions, and applied good basic common sense and common knowledge.

Furthermore, I am a dynamic public speaker; I am a businessman, entrepreneur, and the author of five books thus far; I am working on a sixth book. I only mention these things to let the reader know that I have done my due diligence to render the truth and facts within this book; and to also let the reader know that I am not a lazy man. Laziness is considered a sin. However, my most outstanding asset and quality is that I am a very DYNAMIC public speaker.

Nevertheless, this book is not intended to blame anyone or any

Americans, or to point fingers. It was written with the sole purpose to point out where we as Americans have possibly taken some of the wrong paths and for us to correct our directions; Black and White. But, primarily it was written to get some Black people back on the proper path as some of us seem to be drifting towards hate and malice in race relations and otherwise; which is causing us to miss our blessings from GOD; or causing us to be unable to see or recognize our blessings from GOD; and causing us to be way off balance with our great universe.

Some aspects of this book may have possibly seemed repetitive or redundant. So forgive me for this if that seemed to be the case at certain points. However, as I was writing this book, I did discover that to make sure that my points and messages were thorough and decisive this would be a possibility. I found it necessary to make all of my messages and points clear, thorough, concise, and succinct. And sometimes when one does that it may seem to be somewhat repetitive or redundant at times.

I also made every effort to be as accurate as I could. However, if I made any errors in this book it certainly was not done intentionally, or to mislead, and I ask for your forgiveness and understanding.

Nevertheless, I did my best to educate Americans, more predominantly Black Americans, to bring all Americans closer together and to a higher quality of living within race relations, politics, and all other aspects of American life.

I thank you for reading this book. I hope you enjoyed it and learned something from it. I truly believe America is the epicenter for righteous behavior in the world. This book was created and written by me to educate and to inspire Americans to their highest heights because I believe we have a special role in the divine order of GOD.

AND AGAIN, I STRONGLY FEEL THAT WHEN THE "BAD" OUT-WEIGHS THE "GOOD" IN AMERICA, THE WORLD WILL BE ON A NEVER-ENDING SWIFT DOWNWARD SPIRAL TOWARDS EVIL, DISSENSION, MAYHEM, DISCORD, AND DESTRUCTION.

Please share this book with a friend or family member. May GOD bless you and keep "you" and "your spirit" safe.

By Dr. Ezekiel Fierce Zeke. Dynamic Public Speaker, Educator, Motivator, American Activist, Author, and Actor. Better known as Dr. Zeke, the Educator. My chief employer is GOD.

PURCHASE BOOK & CONTACT INFO.

Buy this book at amazon.com under "Books," "Kindle Store," or "Audible Books & Originals" for Paperback, eBook, or the Virtual Voice Audiobook. Or, buy the audiobook with narration from the AUTHOR PRIMARILY at BarnesandNoble.com, Nook.com, Audiobooks.com, Audiobooksnow.com, and Kobo.com. And possibly buy the audiobook with narration from the AUTHOR at Hoopla, 3 Leaf Group, Bookmate, My Audiobook Library, Bookbeat, Apple, Radish, audible.com, iTunes, Chirp, and many other online audio book retailers & stores and other places.

If you enjoy this book, please leave a 5-star review and/or a comment.

To book me for speaking engagements, comments, & otherwise contact me or my agent at DRZEKE1@PROTONMAIL.COM AND EZEKIELZEKE@PROTONMAIL.COM, &/OR BY MAILING: 2200 ADEN ROAD SUITE #1004, FORT WORTH, TEXAS 76116.

"I LOVE AMERICA."

My six books titled: 1. *THE TRUTH ABOUT BLACKS AND POLICE BRUTALITY. 2. POLICE BRUTALITY?!? MANY BLACK PEOPLE ARE SO CONFUSED! 3. THE TRUTH ABOUT BLACKS AND POLICE-ENCOUNTERS. 4. POLICE-ENCOUNTERS: WHAT BLACK PEOPLE NEED TO KNOW. 5. POLICE BRUTALITY AGAINST BLACKS?!? THE BIG MYTH AND/OR LIE!* and 6. *THE TALK.* All six different books have the same basic exact information and the same exact content. The only differences between these six different books are the book titles and covers. In other words, they are the same exact basic books except for the titles & covers. Also, all chapters and basic information in these six books is also contained in my copyrighted book titled *YES!!! I AM A N.I.G.G.E.R.!!!.* So, if you buy *YES!!! I AM A N.I.G.G.E.R.!!!* once published, you will also have the same basic information that is contained in these six books *as well*, plus the additional information in *YES!!! I AM A N.I.G.G.E.R.!!!.* In other words, basically two books in one.

PIC 130   AND   PIC 134

PIC 125   AND   PIC 127

REFERENCES:

1) All real photos and images in this book are Public Domain and/or Creative Common "CC0" and/or from Pixabay.

2) All clipart images in this book are Public Domain and/or Creative Common "CC0" and/or from Pixabay.

3) THE LIVING BIBLE PARAPHRASED, A THOUGHT-FOR-THOUGHT TRANSLATION, LARGE PRINT EDITION, TYNDALE HOUSE PUBLISHERS, INC., WHEATON, ILLINOIS, COPYRIGHT 1971.

4) Quote from Martin Luther King Jr., Letter from the Birmingham Jail.
https://www.goodreads.com/quotes/tag/civil-disobedience

5) MARTIN LUTHER KING QUOTE PLEASE BE PEACEFUL...
https://christiananimalethics.com/martin-luther-king-jr-quotes/?gclid=CjwKCAiAiarfBRASEiwAw1tYv1vChDu2oF2O17KBC_k-s07a1SuagwZBKbILRk21hDPb3g6rKCLruBoCBG4QAvD_BwE

6) QUOTE FROM MALCOLM X "MESSAGE TO THE GRASS ROOTS," SPEECH, NOV. 1963, DETROIT (PUBLISHED IN MALCOLM X SPEAKS, CH. 1, 1965).
http://malcolmx.com/quotes/
OBEY THE LAW...BUT IF HE PUTS HIS

HANDS ON YOU....

7) "Be peaceful, be courteous." Malcolm X. https://awakenthegreatnesswithin.com/35-inspirational-malcolm-x-quotes-on-success/

8) "We must reject the idea that every time a law's broken, society is guilty rather than the lawbreaker. It is time to restore the American precept that each individual is accountable for his actions."
— Ronald Reagan
https://www.goodreads.com/author/quotes/3543.Ronald_Reagan

9) "Freedom prospers when religion is vibrant and the rule of law under God is acknowledged."
— Ronald Reagan
https://www.goodreads.com/author/quotes/3543.Ronald_Reagan

10) THE TEN GREEN MEN --- MARTIN LUTHER KING JUNIOR, SINGLE GARMENT OF DESTINY, INTERRELATEDNESS.
https://www.weforum.org/agenda/2017/01/7-martin-luther-king-quotes-that-resonate-today/
https://evolutionarycollective.com/tied-together-in-the-single-garment-of-destiny-dr-martin-luther-king-jr-2/

By Dr. Ezekiel Fierce Zeke. Dynamic Public Speaker, Educator, Motivator, American Activist, Author, and Actor. Better known as Dr. Zeke, the Educator. My chief employer is GOD.

PURCHASE BOOK & CONTACT INFO.

Buy this book at amazon.com under "Books," "Kindle Store," or "Audible Books & Originals" for Paperback, eBook, or the Virtual Voice Audiobook. Or, buy the audiobook with narration from the AUTHOR PRIMARILY at BarnesandNoble.com, Nook.com, Audiobooks.com, Audiobooksnow.com, and Kobo.com. And possibly buy the audiobook with narration from the AUTHOR at **Hoopla, 3 Leaf Group**, **Bookmate**, **My Audiobook Library, Bookbeat**, **Apple**, Radish, audible.com, iTunes, Chirp, and many other online audio book retailers & stores and other places.

If you enjoy this book, please leave a 5-star review and/or a comment.

To book me for speaking engagements, comments, & otherwise contact me or my agent at DRZEKE1@PROTONMAIL.COM AND EZEKIELZEKE@PROTONMAIL.COM, &/OR BY MAILING: 2200 ADEN ROAD SUITE #1004, FORT WORTH, TEXAS 76116.

"I LOVE AMERICA."

My six books titled: 1. *THE TRUTH ABOUT BLACKS AND POLICE BRUTALITY. 2. POLICE BRUTALITY?!? MANY BLACK PEOPLE ARE SO CONFUSED! 3. THE TRUTH ABOUT BLACKS AND POLICE-ENCOUNTERS. 4. POLICE-ENCOUNTERS: WHAT BLACK PEOPLE NEED TO KNOW. 5. POLICE BRUTALITY AGAINST BLACKS?!? THE BIG MYTH AND/OR LIE!* and *6. THE TALK*. All six different books have the same basic exact information and the same exact content. The only differences between these six different books are the book titles and covers. In other words, they are the same exact basic books except for the titles & covers. Also, all chapters and basic information in these six books is also contained in my copyrighted book titled *YES!!! I AM A N.I.G.G.E.R.!!!*. So, if you buy *YES!!! I AM A N.I.G.G.E.R.!!!* once published, you will also have the same basic information that is contained in these six books *as well*, plus the additional information in *YES!!! I AM A N.I.G.G.E.R.!!!*. In other words, basically two books in one.

THE TALK

THE TALK

www.ingramcontent.com/pod-product-compliance
Lightning Source LLC
Chambersburg PA
CBHW070348220526
45467CB00001B/295